The Columbia Guide to Online Style

SECOND EDITION

DATE DUE

The Columbia Guide to Online Style

SECOND EDITION

Janice R. Walker and Todd Taylor

 Columbia University Press   New York

Columbia University Press
Publishers Since 1893
New York   Chichester, West Sussex
Copyright © 1998, 2006 Columbia University Press
All rights reserved

Library of Congress Cataloging-in-Publication Data

Walker, Janice R.
    The Columbia guide to online style / Janice R. Walker and
Todd Taylor. — 2nd ed.
        p. cm.
    Includes bibliographical references and index.
    ISBN 0–231–13210–7 (cloth : alk. paper) — 0–231–13211–5 (pbk. : alk. paper) —
    ISBN 0–231–50698–8 (e-book)
    1. Authorship—Data processing—Styles manuals.
    2. Citation of electronic information resources.   I. Taylor, Todd W.
    II. Title.

PN171.F56W35   2006
808′.027—dc22   2006024383

This book is printed on paper with recycled content.
Printed in the United States of America

c 10 9 8 7 6 5 4 3 2 1
p 10 9 8 7 6 5 4 3 2 1

Contents

Figures and Tables

Figures

Tables

Preface

All standards and guides to style, whether aimed at print or other media, necessarily suffer from the problem of trying to regiment the intractable. This book, then, attempts to achieve the apparently impossible: to provide an authoritative guide to the world of online writing and publishing, a world that continues to morph at such a rate that establishing standards may seem impossible or even deplorable. Since the publication of the first edition of *The Columbia Guide to Online Style*, much has changed, especially with respect to the proliferation of electronic or electronically published works. The formats recommended here have not changed substantially, however. What has changed is the need for more and different types of examples and more information to help researchers locate, evaluate, and accurately cite online information.

The variety and complexity of human communication, even within the relatively coordinated realm of academic discourse, seem too vast to be captured or standardized effectively. Furthermore, some argue that standards, rules, and style guides constrict the creative expressions of authors. In fact, many proponents of online writing and electronic publication are specifically encouraged by the prospect that the new media will lead to a radical disruption of the conventions and traditions of print publication. Such arguments are worth noting; however, standards can be as liberating as they are limiting. Not only do conventions and specialized vocabularies provide the utilitarian mechanisms through which communication can take place, they also play a crucial role in simultaneously reflecting, promoting, and defining the values and identity of particular discourse communities. In other words, effective style is not an imposed artifice; it is a product of common values, to the degree that such values can be determined.

Because the spectrum of human communications is vast, this style guide, like others, can address with authority only a small segment of it: the production of academic discourse in the form of student and professional papers and reports and scholarly work for publication either in print or online venues. This book stresses the importance of the connections between style and scholarly integrity, connections on which all academic disciplines rely. Currently, hundreds of published style guides for citing resources and producing texts reflect the particular values and conventions of individual disciplines and specializations within academe. As diverse as these groups may be, however, they all share common concerns. Yet too often manuals present style as a decontextualized catechism of rules to be observed, whereas its primary aim is to promote scholarly integrity and the foundations that allow for new ideas to grow. Many people operate under the misguided notion that style is primarily a means to ensure that authors and publishers receive appropriate intellectual and financial credit for their work and to subjugate initiates in academic discourse, and it would certainly be foolish to deny that such impulses are associated with the promulgation of academic style. Nevertheless, the preeminent goal of style is to support the continuous, communal, and cross-generational process of knowledge building. Style is one important mechanism that helps facilitate this process.

Many have suggested that the mind-boggling explosion of electronic discourse and new media—primarily as the result of word processing, desktop publishing, and Internet technologies—presents a "threat" to scholarly integrity because it promises to upset long-established conventions and traditions. Yet scholarship, scholarly integrity, and style are more likely to shift and become redefined than to evaporate as more and more work is published digitally rather than on paper. In other words, if scholarship is to make a successful transition from print to electronic media, as most believe it will, new standards for ensuring scholarly integrity online must be established.

Tellingly, this book is not so much the result of the authors trying to bottle the ether as much as the ether itself demanding a bottle. In 1994, Janice Walker quietly and somewhat naively developed a simple but highly effective style sheet for citing electronic sources. The style sheet was quickly endorsed by the Alliance for Computers and Writing, became known as the Walker/ACW Style Sheet, and was published on the World Wide Web. Soon after, Walker was bombarded with hundreds of requests from libraries, universities, associations, and publishers for permission to use and duplicate her style sheet. And after the *Chronicle of Higher Education, Internet World, USA Today*, and *Newsweek* featured the Walker/ACW style sheet in their publications, countless writers, scholars, and researchers contacted her, encouraging her to expand this work.

Because of the simplicity of creating and storing information on the World Wide Web as well as the global accessibility it offers, online publishing seems to have arrived at a period of relative stability, at least in the sense that even though technology continues to change daily, the World Wide Web provides the first glimpse of an infrastructure that promises to support reasonable levels of online scholarly integrity. Clearly, much remains to be done if most new research and scholarship is one day to be published online. One major obstacle is the reliability of the infrastructure. Who is going to ensure that the Internet is stable and reliable and not a nightmare of bottlenecks? Will corporations or governments provide such reliability? Who will organize, index, and provide long-term archives for online scholarship? Will university libraries supply these services? Who will oversee the prudent evolution of other mechanisms important to online scholarly integrity, such as peer review? Will university presses and journal editors do this work?

Even while such questions are being answered, we can begin establishing and promoting standards for the production of conventional academic publications through electronic media, standards that should help support the eventual development of reliable infrastructures. Two important caveats regarding such standards must be addressed, however. First, even though this book is a guide to more or less traditional forms of scholarship published online, or at least using online sources, scholars should at least consider exploring experimental forms that fall outside the scope of our project. Experiments in online publishing such as hypertextual indexes and interactive footnotes already demonstrate some of the ways online documents can greatly improve on conventional print-oriented styles. Refusing to encourage and take advantage of such experiments is clearly more a threat to scholarly integrity than is the migration of scholarship from print to electronic publishing.

The second caveat speaks to the style of this book itself. At first it may seem that this guide to online style is bound by the limitations of print publishing, and in a sense that is true. How can the reader expect to rely on the standards it describes given that electronic publishing technologies may change even as this book is in press or between editions? The answer is that the core standards promoted in this book—for citing most online resources, providing in-text citations, and for producing electronic documents— will not change dramatically in most cases. That is, while how we access scholarly works in a digital age and how we determine the elements we need to adequately create, disseminate, and reference these works may change dramatically in years to come, the elements themselves remain. While we cannot hope to address all of the questions the future of scholarly publishing in a digital age may prompt, a list of Frequently Asked Questions (FAQs) is available on the Web site for this book at http://www.columbia.edu/cu/cup/cgos, along with a link to email the authors with questions we have not yet considered.

The authors wish to acknowledge the departments of English at the University of South Florida, Tampa, and the University of North Carolina, Chapel Hill, and the Department of Writing and Linguistics at Georgia Southern University for their support. We also want to thank Jennifer Crewe at Columbia University Press and her anonymous reviewers for their enormous help developing the manuscript and preparing this book. And, of course, this book would not be possible without the questions, suggestions, and challenges from literally thousands of students, teachers, and other researchers who have driven the authors to continue expanding this work. A special thanks goes to the Office of Research and Sponsored Services at Georgia Southern University for their financial support of this publication.

We would also like to note that this book is truly a coauthored work, with both Janice Walker and Todd Taylor contributing equally to its development and publication. However, since one name inevitably had to precede the other, the authors agreed that Walker's name should be listed first because she had already established the "Walker/ACW Style for Citation of Electronic Sources" before the authors decided to write this book; the term "first author" does not apply to this book in any other sense.

The Columbia Guide to Online Style

SECOND EDITION

Part 1

Locating and Citing Source Materials

RESEARCH IN THE ELECTRONIC AGE

The starting point for most research is no longer the library but the **World Wide Web**. To some, this statement may seem heretical; to others, however, it is merely descriptive: students today are likely to begin any research project by using a **search engine** to locate material, often with tragic results.

The problem is twofold. First, knowing where to search for reliable information on a given topic is complicated by the chaotic and shifting nature of the World Wide Web. Like trying to hit a moving target, locating sources on the **Internet** can be frustrating, unreliable, and erratic. Sites move or disappear with alarming frequency, while new ones are constantly emerging. Researchers often find that even with the advantages of electronic search capabilities—the speed with which information in vast **databases** can be searched, for example—finding useful sources is time consuming and sometimes downright impossible.

Second, many electronically published sources, especially those published on the Web, do not provide enough information to evaluate or cite them adequately. That is, while we can ascertain much about the authority of a print source from its imprint—university press or scholarly, peer-reviewed journal, etc.—a **Web site** may provide few if any clues to its author, sources, currency, or sponsorship. What clues there are may be difficult to determine without some knowledge of the increasingly transparent **protocols** that enable Web authoring and publishing in the first place.

Further complicating the dilemma faced by researchers in the dawn of the twenty-first century is the move toward more and more **online** publication of "traditional" scholarship, especially in the face of severe financial constraints faced by many university presses. While online databases that provide full-text or full-image articles and online-only—or online counterparts of for-print—scholarly journals are a boon to knowledgeable researchers, the result of so much wealth is daunting. The sheer volume of information available online makes it virtually impossible for anyone to know at any given time what's "out there" and even more difficult to know where to begin looking for it.

In part 1, we present information to guide researchers in their quest for sources, helping them locate information and carefully evaluate it. Where to look for information, we argue, depends first and foremost on the type of information needed—and more and more of this information can now be located online. However, because the online world is still (and we hope will remain) a space with relatively little regulation, we also provide guidelines for evaluating information sources. These guidelines should help the reader come to a better understanding of citation practices as an integral part of research and writing, not only as a way to avoid charges of plagiarism or to fulfill some vague classroom dictates but as central to the act of knowledge building, the bricks and mortar, as it were, in the construction of a given rhetorical act. Thus, we present five principles of citation style as a foundation upon which to build a solid structure.

This second edition of *The Columbia Guide to Online Style* includes two full chapters of models—one for humanities-style projects (i.e., MLA), and one for scientific-style (i.e., APA), each chapter offering more models than ever before for both in-text and bibliographic formats, covering a wide variety of types of electronic and electronically accessed sources, including those most often being used by students and other researchers in this digital age.

Part 2 of this book offers some suggestions for authors and publishers for issues of document production both in print and online for the digital age, for example, responding to changes in standard **markup languages** and document formats, document-production software, and the proliferation of **multimedia** publication, including guidelines for basic Web site architecture.

Our intent is not to fix a moment in time by prescribing rigid formulae; instead, we hope to suggest ways to ensure that researchers in a digital world will have the information necessary to adequately locate and evaluate scholarly sources. However, there is no guarantee that authors or publishers will follow these suggestions. The very nature of the World Wide Web, in fact, guarantees that no one standard is likely to be enforceable anytime in the near future. It is thus incumbent on researchers themselves to learn to locate reliable information, to evaluate the information they find, and to document the sources they use as fully and as accurately as the information allows.

1.1. LOCATING INFORMATION

Knowing where to look for information depends to a large extent on the type of information needed. Scholarly projects usually rely on rigorous, peer-reviewed sources (see table 1.1). While many of these scholarly sources *are* now available online, of course, with many more migrating to **digital** forms every day, print sources still provide a wealth of information that researchers cannot afford to overlook. Nowadays, locating print sources does not necessarily mean leaving home (or leaving the World Wide Web), since most university libraries now offer students and faculty access to the library catalog, online databases, and many other reference sources through the library's **home page** on the World Wide Web. Nonetheless, knowing where to start a search—whether to begin with the library's home page or an Internet search engine, for instance—requires an understanding of what different types of sources have to offer a researcher as well as where best to locate them. Obviously, the library may not be the best place to look for up-to-the-minute information. Alternatively, the World Wide Web will usually not be the best possible source for finding extended, analytical work on scholarly topics.

TABLE 1.1 Assessing Sources

Types of Sources	Authority	Current?	Stable?	Publication Medium
Scholarly books and articles	Written by experts. Rigorously peer-reviewed. Published by university or scholarly press. Articles are included in scholarly journals or anthologized in collections. Scrupulous attention to documentation of sources.	No. Although scholarly articles are generally more current than book publications, both are time consuming to produce. Hence, scholarly books and articles do not usually represent the most current work in the field.	Yes, usually.	Books are usually available only in print; however, some scholarly books are available on CD-ROM or online. As copyrights expire and works go into the public domain, many scholarly works are being digitized and may be freely available on the World Wide Web. Articles in scholarly journals and book collections are indexed by scholarly databases

TABLE 1.1 Assessing Sources (*continued*)

Types of Sources	Authority	Current?	Stable?	Publication Medium
				(see appendix A). Some of these databases offer full-text or full-image versions of these articles, in addition to providing bibliographic citations to enable locating the articles in the university library. Some scholarly journals are also published on the World Wide Web. These journals may require a fee for subscription access. Many university libraries provide free access to these resources for students and faculty.
Serious books and articles	Written by experts or professional writers. Reviewed by editors and/or peers. Published by commercial press. Documentation of sources may not be as scrupulous as for more scholarly works.	Usually more current than scholarly books or articles.		Serious books and articles, like scholarly works, may be indexed by scholarly databases (see appendix A). Some of these databases offer full-text or full-image versions of these articles, in addition to providing bibliographic information. The works may also be

(continued)

TABLE 1.1 Assessing Sources (*continued*)

Types of Sources	Authority	Current?	Stable?	Publication Medium
				available on CD-ROM or online. Many library home pages offer links or access to these publications
Popular magazines	Written by professional writers or journalists. Reviewed by editors. Published by commercial press. Informal documentation of sources.	Usually current, but sometimes at the expense of in-depth coverage.	Usually	Usually available in print, on CD-ROM, or online, sometimes for free, sometimes by subscription. Articles in many popular magazines are indexed by databases such as *Readers' Guide Abstracts* (see appendix A), and some may offer full-text or full-image versions of articles.
Newspapers	Written by journalists. Reviewed by editors. Published by commercial press. Informal documentation of sources.	Usually current.	Usually.	Many newspapers offer both print and online editions. Major newspapers are indexed by scholarly databases such as *Lexis-Nexis* (see appendix A), or may be searchable through the newspaper's Web site. Archives of

TABLE 1.1 Assessing Sources (*continued*)

Types of Sources	Authority	Current?	Stable?	Publication Medium
Sponsored Web sites	Authorship varies, from experts to professional writers and journalists to individuals. Information may be reviewed by the sponsor or publisher to ensure its suitability for the sponsor's purpose. Sponsoring organizations may include commercial ventures, nonprofit organizations, government agencies, religious organizations, educational institutions, or special-interest groups. Documentation of sources varies depending on the type of site and its sponsorship	While Web sites do allow for up-to-the-minute reporting of information, not all are updated on a regular basis.	Varies. Some Web sites regularly archive articles for later retrieval; others simply disappear.	articles are often available online (World Wide Web). Some library databases include bibliographic information on selected Web sites, and some of the more useful sites may be linked from the library home page.

(continued)

TABLE 1.1 Assessing Sources (*continued*)

Types of Sources	Authority	Current?	Stable?	Publication Medium
Individual Web sites and home pages	Authors vary greatly—they may be experts, professional writers or journalists, or students. Anyone with access can publish a page on the World Wide Web. Pages are usually not reviewed. Documentation varies widely depending on the author's purpose and intended audience.	Varies. While individual Web pages may be capable of offering the most current information available, they may not be updated or maintained.	Varies. Some individual Web sites are archived and relatively stable, but most offer no guarantees.	Online (World Wide Web).
Interviews and chats	The authority of interviews and chats depends on the speakers. Interviews and chat conversations with experts in a field can be very reliable and illuminating; however, since the speakers do not have the time to care-	Yes.	No.	Multiple, ranging from text or HTML (e.g., MOO or instant messenger transcripts and personal email) to audio and/or video transcripts.

TABLE 1.1 Assessing Sources (*continued*)

Types of Sources	Authority	Current?	Stable?	Publication Medium
	fully consider their words, include documentation of sources, or to revise and edit for publication, these conversations do not carry the same weight as a published book or article by the same person.			
Listservs and newsgroups	Most newsgroups allow anyone to post; authors may therefore run the gamut from students or interested laypersons to experts. Listservs, which usually require subscriptions, may be moderated or unmoderated; they may include more serious discussion; or they may, like newsgroups, allow anyone	Yes.	Sometimes depending on whether the postings are archived.	Text or HTML.

(continued)

TABLE 1.1 Assessing Sources (*continued*)

Types of Sources	Authority	Current?	Stable?	Publication Medium
	with an interest in the topic to post. Like interviews and chat conversations, authors do not usually take the time to document and revise their postings, so these postings, too, do not usually carry the same weight as published books or articles.			
Blogs and wikis	Authors vary, from individuals personal ruminations to serious journalists, researchers, and others contributing to a scholarly compilation. Postings may be reviewed or updated by subsequent readers. Source information may be documented, linked, or omitted.	Varies.	Sometimes.	Multiple formats; online.

TABLE 1.1 Assessing Sources (*continued*)

Types of Sources	Authority	Current?	Stable?	Publication Medium
Databases	Varies; however most articles indexed or included in library databases carry the same authority as print articles. Other online databases may include a wide variety of types of sources, some questionable, others more reliable.	Varies.	Usually.	Online (World Wide Web); intranet; library portal; CD-ROM.

1.1.1. Search Library Catalogs

Online **library catalogs** offer researchers a means to locate scholarly books, journals, and other media quickly and efficiently. Nowadays, most college and university library catalogs, such as the one shown in figure 1.1 from the University of South Florida, are accessible on the World Wide Web, often through the library's home page, and allow for searches by author, title, subject, **keywords**, or other identifiers.

It is often possible to search catalogs at other institutions as well, across the street or across the world, to locate material not owned by a local library (see appendix A for a partial list of library holdings that can be freely searched on the World Wide Web).

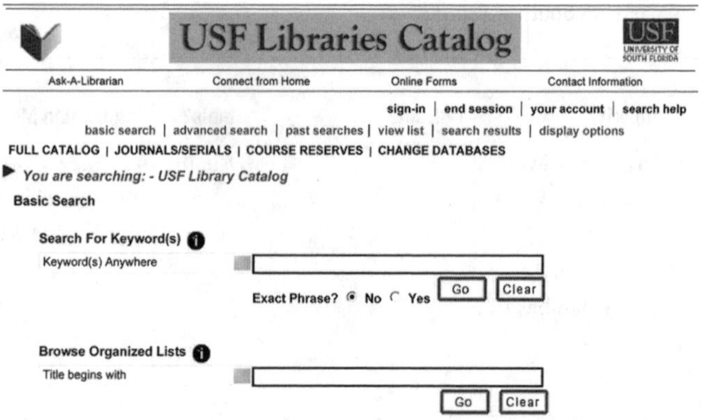

FIGURE 1.1 The University of South Florida Library catalog.
Source: http://sf.aleph.fcla.edu/F?RN=857882890.

A library catalog search will usually provide bibliographic information about library holdings, including the author, title, publication information, location, status (whether or not the work is checked out), and more, as shown in figure 1.2.

1.1.2. Search Online Databases

Searching databases such as *Dissertation Abstracts/Digital Dissertations at ProQuest*, the *MLA Bibliography*, or *Academic Search Premier* can help researchers locate material housed almost anywhere in the world. Many libraries offer access to a number of powerful online databases, either through their home page or on **CD-ROM**. Once you have located the bibliographic information, you can determine whether your library owns the material by searching the library's catalog of holdings. Some databases will locate the material for you or provide full-text or full-image copies online (full-text **files** do not usually include illustrations or page breaks; full-image resources offer exact copies

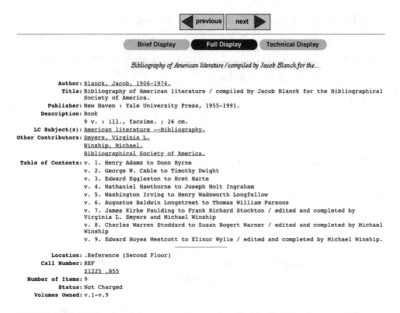

FIGURE 1.2 Bibliographic entry from the Zach S. Henderson Library, Georgia Southern University.

Source: http://library.georgiasouthern.edu/.

of original material, including pictures, pagination, etc.). If your library does not own the material, you may be able to order print copies through interlibrary loan, a program that allows member institutions to borrow materials from other member institutions throughout the world, often at no charge. Check with your library for more information. See appendix A for a list of selected databases, available either online, through your library's Web **portal**, or on CD-ROM.

1.1.3. Search the World Wide Web

There are many different Internet search engines, each with its own peculiarities. Nonetheless, most of them use similar type search queries, usually plain English keywords. Moreover, many search engines and online databases also allow for more advanced **Boolean searches**. Table 1.2 illustrates some common **Boolean operators** and how to use them.

TABLE 1.2 Using Boolean Search Terms.

Term	Description
AND	Limits your search to only those documents that contain both terms, in any order. For example, **death AND penalty**
OR	Searches for all instances of either term in documents. For example, **death OR penalty**
NOT	Eliminates terms from your search so that documents containing the term will not be listed. For example, **death AND penalty NOT animals**
" "	Groups words together and searches for them as phrases in a document. For example, **"death penalty"**
[ ]	Nesting search terms allows for greater flexibility in combining operators. For example, [**"death penalty"** AND **"supreme court"**] NOT **animals**
+	A plus sign (+) before each term ensures that each term will be searched for. For example, **+death +penalty**
-	The minus sign ("-") will exclude terms from the search. For example, **+death -penalty**
*	Asterisks (*) allow for "wild card" searching, that is, searches that include all forms of a word or all types of a file. For example, to search for documents that contain the word "penalty" as well as the plural form, "penalties," use **penalt***

Different search engines may search different types of sites; thus, if you do not find what you are looking for with one, try a different one. Appendix A includes a list of selected search engines and directories, as well as a list of online collections and general reference sources. Keep in mind that the Internet is constantly changing, so the results you obtain on one day may be quite different on another. Keep a record of important Internet **addresses** and, for citation purposes, you may also want to keep a record of the date you accessed the sites along with other pertinent information, such as author(s)'s name(s), titles, search terms, etc.

1.2. EVALUATING SOURCES

Most scholarly work published in print formats has undergone a thorough review process by editors and knowledgeable peers (see table 1.1 on page 6). Unfortunately, other types of sources—both print and electronic—may not be held to the same high standards. Of course, even scholarly publications may become outdated, with information or claims overturned or questioned by subsequent scholars. Researchers must carefully evaluate *all* of the sources on which they rely in order to ensure the credibility of their own work.

For print sources, the author(s), title, and publication information are generally easy to locate: the title page of a book, for instance, will generally provide most of this information. For Internet sources, however, it may be difficult or even impossible to determine some or even most of the information necessary to evaluate a given source adequately. Nonetheless, researchers are responsible to their readers for determining the reliability of the information on which they base their claims. If a source cannot be substantiated, therefore, researchers may need to locate additional sources either to replace the questionable one or to verify the information it contains. At any rate, determining such features of a source as its authority, currency, and relevance is as important—and sometimes as frustrating—as locating the source in the first place.

1.2.1. Authority

A primary indication of a work's authority is usually vested in its authorship. That is, the credentials of the author(s) lend credibility to the work itself. Consider whether or not the author has education or training in the field, experience, or other factors that lend credence to the work. When no author is listed, as may be the case for some Web sites, look for information about corporate or organizational authors or sponsorship, editors, compilers, or others responsible for the information contained in the source. Check for "About the Author" or "About Us" links, copyright statements (often located at the bottom of a Web page), or **metatags** in the **source code** itself, or examine the **Uniform Resource Locator (URL)** for information, as shown in table 1.3.

The *protocol* represents an agreed-upon means of communication between computers on the Internet. The most common protocol for Web sites and the default in most Web **browsers** is "http://" or **Hypertext Transfer Protocol**. Other protocols include "ftp://" (**File Transfer Protocol**), "telnet://" (**telnet** usually requires access to a telnet **client** on the user's home computer), "mailto:" (a pro-

TABLE 1.3 Understanding URLs

Protocol	Domain	Directory	Subdirectories	File Name	File Extension
http://	www.columbia.edu/	cu/	cup/cgos/	index	.html
http://	infotrac.galenet.com/	menu/		index	.html
http://	www.dublincore.org/	about/	copyright/	index	.html

tocol that directs an **email** client to automatically open and send a message to the given email address), and "news:" (a protocol for accessing **newsgroups** on the Internet). The computer that hosts a site is indicated by the *domain*. For example, "www.columbia.edu" is the World Wide Web **server** (www) for Columbia University (columbia), an educational institution (edu). More information is provided by the *directories* and *subdirectories*: the "cu" **directory** contains (or "serves") the Columbia University Web pages; "cup" is the **subdirectory** for Columbia University Press; and "cgos" houses the Web files for *The Columbia Guide to Online Style*. When no *file name* is given in the URL, Web browsers default to the index. html file; otherwise, the Web browser will look for a specific file name if included. The *file extension* tells the Web browser the type of **software** needed to access the file (e.g., .html files are handled by Web browser software, .doc and .wpd files by specific types of **word processors**, and .pdf files by Adobe Acrobat Reader). For more information on **file extensions**, see appendix B.

The extension included in the **domain name** indicates the type of organization that **hosts** the Web site. Some of the more common domain extensions and a sample of country codes are listed in table 1.4.

The extensions listed in table 1.4 do not automatically add to or detract from a site's credibility, of course. An educational institution may host sponsored sites, but it will also usually host many individual and student sites, for which the institution is not responsible. Likewise, many commercial sites host individual pages (for instance, http://geocities.yahoo.com allows members to publish Web pages for free), some of which may represent scholarly projects but most of which represent individual interests.

Finally, a two-letter country designation may be included, indicating a server located outside of the United States (the .us designation is seldom used). For example, the domain "www.unimelb. edu.au" indicates the World Wide Web server for the University of Melbourne, an educational institution in Australia. For a list of

TABLE 1.4 Domain Extensions and Country Designators

Domains		Countries	
.com	Commercial	.au	Australia
.edu	Institutional	.ca	Canada
.gov	Government	.jp	Japan
.mil	Military	nz	New Zealand
.net	Network site	.uk	United Kingdom
.org	Organization	.us	United States

country codes and domain extensions, see http://www.webopedia. com/quick_ref/topleveldomains/countrycodeA-E.asp. Ultimately, the final test of authority resides in careful reading. A reliable source is usually one that is logically organized, with few if any grammatical errors, and with working links and graphics. Any facts or figures should be current and carefully documented (see table 1.1 on page 00), and claims made by the author should be substantiated with verifiable evidence. Look for a link or information to contact the author or organization responsible for the site as well.

1.2.2. Currency

Generally, researchers prefer to rely on the most current works in their field. Look for publication dates, dates of last modification or revision, or copyright dates on a Web page or electronic publication. Some online **serials** may include publication dates in the URL, or metatags in the document source code may provide additional publication information (see figure 1.3).

Another possible source of information can be found in "About this Site" links. Or try "moving up" the URL by deleting the file name and subdirectories, one at a time, to try to locate additional information. For example, the Web page at http://www.geocities. com/boudicca_1960/Guinevere.html provides no information

FIGURE 1.3 Locating publication dates.

Source: http://www.nytimes.com/2006/03/09/technology/09tablet.html.

about the author of the site. Deleting the file name, Guinevere. html, however, takes us to http://www.geocities.com/boudicca_ 1960, where we learn that the page is "A Forum for Discussing Writing, Literature, Music, Movies, Myths, and More." This page also contains an "About Me" **link** where we learn that the author is a teacher and writer. An email link to the author is provided if we need more information. Be careful, however; removing the "boudicca_1960" directory will take us to the Geocities home page, which is not responsible for the Web sites published by its members.

If all else fails, contact the author or organization responsible for a site. Check to make sure links on the page still work (broken links may be an indication of a page which has not been updated in some time), and read through the work with a critical eye (a source that refers to the World Trade Center as "the tallest skyscraper in the world," for example, would obviously have been written prior to the events of September 2001, as well as before the erection of the Petronas Towers in 1998 and the Sears Tower in 1974).

If you are not able to verify the publication or last revision date of a source, you may need to verify any facts or figures it contains or any important claims it makes by locating other recent work to substantiate them.

1.2.3. Relevance

Merely including sources unnecessarily to pad a works cited or references list can actually work against a researcher, of course. Consider whether the work is directly relevant to a project. Look for sources that answer important questions and support your own claims or, alternatively, that present counterclaims or arguments that need to be addressed. Sources may also present useful examples or illustrations of important points.

Powerful electronic search capabilities often provide researchers with an overabundance of possible sources. For example, a

Google search for "George Washington" returns as many as 64,000,000 hits. Many, if not most, of these hits will not be relevant for a research project about George Washington's childhood, for instance. Use Boolean operators (see table 1.2 on page 16) to combine **search terms** to narrow the focus of the search. Carefully review what's left to determine what the sources will contribute to the project. Even the most authoritative and up-to-date sources are worthless if they do not contribute something of value.

1.2.4. Other Considerations

Careful reading can reveal more information about a source that should be considered when evaluating its usefulness and authority. Consider the author's purpose in writing; for instance: Is the author's purpose apparent or explicit? Can you detect any biases that may affect the author's choice to present or omit facts or ideas? Does the author's choice of audience or **medium** (a Web page versus a print document or **Portable Document Format (PDF)** file, for instance) affect the presentation? Consider, too, if the person or organization who created the Web page or document advocates a particular point of view. Is the information presented in a balanced way? That is, does the author or organization treat opposing viewpoints fairly? If the site is a commercial one, does it attempt to sell something? If so, the information presented on the site may or may not be impartial. Look out for humor or satire a well; do not mistake tongue-in-cheek information for fact.

1.3. AVOIDING PLAGIARISM

To many teachers and scholars, plagiarism is the ultimate sin. Plagiarism is the act of presenting the work or ideas of others as your own. Intentional plagiarism is just plain dishonest and unethical, of course. Turning in a paper written by someone else with your name on it, for example, can be cause for failure or even expulsion from some schools. More prevalent than such intentional dishonesty, however, is unintentional plagiarism—failure to adequately cite not only exact quotations but also paraphrases and summaries, information, and ideas obtained from outside sources. Luckily, most unintentional plagiarism can be avoided quite easily simply by careful note taking and an understanding of the purpose of citation practices beyond the strictures of plagiarism (see chapter 2). For more information, see "Defining and Avoiding Plagiarism: The WPA Statement on Best Practices" at http://wpacouncil.org/node/9.

1.3.1. Take Careful Notes

Take careful note of information obtained from any source, electronic or print, to facilitate citation and to avoid unintentional plagiarism. Carefully note exact quotations, whether you write them out or copy and paste them from an online source, including the exact location from which you obtained them. Include citation information in your notes for ideas, facts and figures, and illustrations or other multimedia material as well.

Many researchers still use index cards to take notes, keyed to bibliographic cards that provide all the information necessary to create a works cited or references list. Other researchers make notes on photocopies or printouts of sources. You may create a simple database or separate word-processed file to keep track of information as well. Many online library catalogs and databases allow bibliographic records to be **downloaded** and saved or printed out, or you may copy and paste bibliographic information directly into your word-processed document. "**Bookmarks**" or "**Favorites**" files in most Web browsers (see figure 1.4) allow users to save and retrieve locations online and organize the information they find, but these may not be useful for researchers who need access to files when they are not connected to the World Wide Web.

Saving **Web pages** to **disk** or other storage media for **offline** access is a dangerous practice, since the saved file may not include important information, such as the URL needed to access the original site. Graphics, links, and other important information may also be missing from saved files. Printouts of Web pages may include most of this information, but some Web sites can be lengthy. Consider printing out only the first page of important sites, being sure to include the URL and noting the date of access.

1.3.2. Consider Using Bibliography Software

Bibliography software may work within your Web browser or word processor and can help to simplify record keeping by automatically keying your notes to the bibliographic record of the source. Programs such as *RefWorks* are Web-based and work across platforms, allowing users to create a database of online resources automatically, and some bibliographic software, such as the one in figure 1.5, will even format citations for you. Be careful, however; bibliography software can sometimes cause difficulties for editors and publishers. For more information on preparing manuscripts to submit for publication, see part 2.

The resulting bibliographic entries are only as good as the information provided by the user, of course. Even software that offers to capture the information from the Web will not necessarily locate all of the necessary information for you, and URLs may need to be checked carefully (many databases and searchable sites create URLs "on the fly," with the result that the URL is useless for reaccessing the site). For more information on citing sources, see chapter 2.

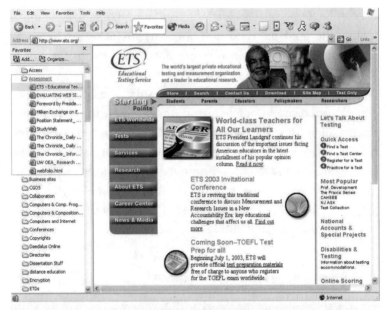

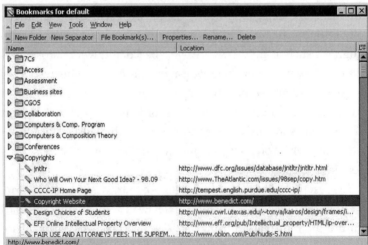

FIGURE 1.4 Internet Explorer's Favorites file and Netscape's Bookmarks file.

Source: Microsoft Internet Explorer 6.0, © 1995–2001 Microsoft Corp. Netscape Communicator 7.1, © 2000–2003 Netscape Communications Corporation.

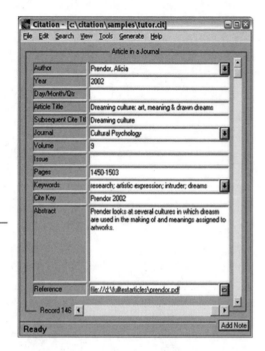

You can enter as many keywords as you need, as well as a summary of the work - and a link to related documents or websites.

FIGURE 1.5 Bibliographic software can automatically format your citations.
Source: Oberon Development. http://www.citationonline.net.

1.4. DOCUMENTING SOURCES

Ethical researchers pay scrupulous attention to documenting the source of words and ideas borrowed from others, not only to avoid charges of plagiarism but also to lend additional support to their own work. Understanding the elements of citation and the logic behind documentation practices can help readers determine the credibility of sources on which an author has relied and can help an author determine the information necessary for documenting most types of source material. Chapter 2 explains the logic on which citation practices are based and presents five principles of citation for both print-based and electronically accessed sources to help determine what information needs to be cited and how to cite it.

2

THE LOGIC OF CITATION

Citation is the practice of systematically indicating the origins of thoughts, ideas, knowledge, or words that one uses to author a report, essay, article, speech, book, Web site, or other work. The key to understanding the logic behind citation lies in understanding the systems upon which it is based. Those who believe the primary purpose of citation is to monitor and police authors misunderstand the logic of the practice. Many have learned to perceive citation as a series of difficult rules employed solely to counter plagiarism, to ensure that authors and publishers of original work receive proper intellectual and financial credit for their work, and even to subjugate new initiates in the world of academic writing. And in all fairness, such misperceptions are not completely the fault of those who see citation in such a negative light. To date, most guides to academic style have not done a good job of explaining *how* to cite in terms of *why* one should do so.

The big picture, however, is about knowledge building: each piece of reported research adds to the collective construction of knowledge. Research serves as the foundation on which new contributions to knowledge are built. Without citation, there is no reliable and organized system for knowledge building, no mortar for securing the foundation. Knowledge building is, of course, not as straightforward as stacking bricks. If academic knowledge were a building, the structure would be impressive indeed, but—far from being flawless, complete, or symmetrical—its parts would be constantly crumbling and being rebuilt, with scores of different construction crews with different architectural styles and blueprints at work on different parts at the same time.

The primary reason for citation is that it encourages and supports the organized accumulation of academic knowledge. Consider, for example, the fact that most scholars approach bibliographies more in terms of the knowledge they generate than the strictures they enforce. Most academic writers will be familiar with the concept of *bibliography* in the most general sense of the term. A bibliography is a list of works that a writer has consulted in the creation of a new work. In its most familiar format, this list is usually found at the end of an academic document. Scholars—the people most actively involved in academic knowledge building—often read bibliographies with as much interest as they study the work itself because bibliographies and citations contain crucial information that generates additional opportunities in the pursuit of knowledge building. Of course, one cannot expect that all writers, especially students, will immediately learn to read and appreciate bibliographies as experienced or full-time scholars do. But inexperienced writers are more likely to comprehend, appreciate, use, and possibly even master citation if they understand its primary purpose.

This discussion may seem remedial to those who have been in the business of research and scholarship for years. However, online scholarship quite simply hasn't been around long enough for many of us to have developed the deeply ingrained intuitions that are at work in the world of print scholarship. With few exceptions, that is, online scholarship adds further complications because of the distinct difficulties imposed on researchers by the lack of standards for many types of online sources. Changing technology thus requires us to focus attention on the origins of citation, which have become blurred by years of mere replication without sincere interrogation into the practices of our predecessors in academic discourse.

2.1. FIVE PRINCIPLES OF CITATION STYLE

Understanding citation style and practices depends on understanding the principles on which it is based—access, intellectual property, economy, standardization, and transparency.

2.1.1. The Principle of Access

Citation styles help readers locate original documents to which authors have referred in preparing their own work. The principle of access has many ramifications. Access is valuable so that readers can make use of and build on the sources that an author has discovered; it helps readers evaluate the author's reliability by allowing them to examine the contexts from which the author selected citations. Part of evaluating an author's reliability is being able to verify that work has been cited appropriately and credit has not been taken for ideas or research established by someone else. Subcorollaries under the principle of access require that citation style not just facilitate access but do so with a high degree of efficiency. For many types of electronic sources, providing the Internet address, or URL, will accomplish this purpose, but often the address alone is not sufficient. Electronic sources move or disappear entirely; search engines or databases serve up information with addresses that may—or may not—allow direct access; and **frames** or other coding may confuse the actual location of the information being cited. In order to ensure that the principle of access is adhered to, then, citations of these sources must include as much information as possible within the limits of what a researcher can reasonably be expected to ascertain.

2.1.2. The Principle of Intellectual Property

Using someone else's ideas, words and phrases, or form of presentation without giving proper credit is plagiarism and can carry serious academic as well as legal penalties. Our conception of plagiarism is based on the notion of ownership of intellectual property. In the United States, the logic behind the principle of intellectual property is based on an economic model, stemming from the Constitution's call to "promote the Progress of Science and useful Arts, by securing for limited Times to Authors and Inventors the exclusive Right to their respective Writings and Discoveries" (art. 1, sec. 8). Under federal copyright law, words and their form of presentation must be "fixed" in order to be copyrightable. Ideas themselves cannot be copyrighted; only their embodiment has economic value. Beyond intellectual property laws, however, are considerations of ethics. Authors give credit for ideas borrowed from others as part of the process of knowledge building; we build upon—or refute—the ideas of others. In turn, our own ideas may become the foundation or building blocks for future work. Additionally, we give credit in the form of citation when we use the ideas of others simply because it is right to do so, thereby adding to our own credibility and authority as scholars.

Electronic sources, of course, come in a variety of forms, including electronic copies of print-based work, digital graphics, video and audio files, software, Web pages (both fixed and those created on demand), and more. Much of the confusion concerning how intellectual property laws relate to these sources centers on the question of the fixity of the medium. Regardless of how these laws eventually come to be applied, researchers need to be scrupulous in their citations in order to ensure the credibility of their own work. Thus, standards of citation should govern in this medium just as in any other wherein the principle of intellectual property must be honored.

2.1.3. The Principle of Economy

Citation style should include as much information as necessary and yet be as brief as possible so readers can quickly grasp the information they need and publishers can conserve costs incurred in terms of paper, ink, and time. The following approach to citation obviously violates the principle of economy:

> The passage I quote is from an excellent book titled entitled *The Center Will Hold: Critical Perspectives on Writing Center Scholarship.* The book was edited by Michael A. Pemberton and Joyce Kinkead. The passage I cite was located in the chapter, "Power and Authority in Peer Tutoring"; Peter Carino authored the chapter. This chapter can be found on pages 96 through 113. The book was published in 2003 by Utah State University Press, which is located in Logan, Utah, if you need to contact them.

This example is clearly annoying, a waste of time and space as compared with a conventional citation containing similar information.

Following the principle of economy both of the following citation styles reduce a potentially lengthy explanation to its essential elements, following a code whereby important information such as the title of a book, the name of its editor, and the pages on which a particular chapter is located is indicated through formatting.

MLA Style

Author's full name   Title of chapter or article in quotation marks, with first word and all major words capitalized.

Title of book in italics, capitalizing first word and all major words

Name(s) of editor(s) for anthologies or collections

Place of publication   Publisher   Year of Publication   Pages numbers of chapter or article

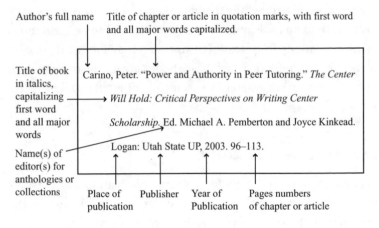

Carino, Peter. "Power and Authority in Peer Tutoring." *The Center Will Hold: Critical Perspectives on Writing Center Scholarship.* Ed. Michael A. Pemberton and Joyce Kinkead. Logan: Utah State UP, 2003. 96–113.

APA Style

Author's last name and initial(s)   Year of Publication   Title of article or chapter, capitalizing first word and any proper nouns

Name(s) of editor(s) and type of contribution

Title of book in italics, capitalizing only the first word, proper nouns, and the first word after a colon

Page numbers of article   Place of publication   Publisher

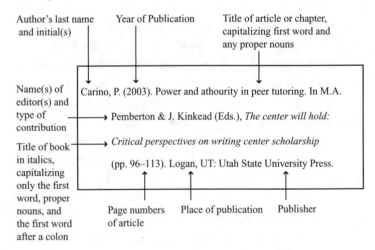

Carino, P. (2003). Power and athourity in peer tutoring. In M.A. Pemberton & J. Kinkead (Eds.), *The center will hold: Critical perspectives on writing center scholarship* (pp. 96–113). Logan, UT: Utah State University Press.

Formatting can be defined as the typographical arrangement and appearance of textual elements: the physical appearance of letters and words on a page, screen, surface, and so on. The most common devices used to format citations are punctuation, font style, and ordering of elements. The use of punctuation in the form of quotation marks placed around a title in humanities styles, for example, is a formatting code that usually tells the reader that what is enclosed is the title of an essay, article, or chapter. Using italics as opposed to a normal font style is a code that typically indicates the title of a journal, report, or book. The placement of the name of the editor of a book is also a code, indicating that the editor is not the author of the chapter cited.

2.1.4. The Principle of Standardization

A comparison between the lengthy prose citation and the codified citations above also explains a fourth corollary of citation style: authors and readers must both understand the code being used; therefore that code must be standardized. Consider, for example, the following codified message:

Columbia University Press
61 W. 62 St.
New York, NY 10023

The standardization of this code allows everyone to understand its meaning. We all know that this is a mailing address and that Columbia University Press is the addressee, which can receive mail sent to a building numbered 61 on West Sixty-second Street in the city of New York in the state of New York, and that the five-digit ZIP code helps postal services deliver mail to that address more efficiently.

Like citation style, the code for indicating a mailing address makes use of abbreviations, punctuation, formatting, and ordering. It is so widely recognized because it always follows explicit standards.

In the same way, if authors and readers are to use citation style to support effective knowledge building, they must understand and employ the standards on which the codified style is based. Unfortunately, there is no one "right" way to format a citation. Standards depend on the discipline in which an author works (e.g., humanities-based or scientific-based disciplines) and the type of source being cited. That is, the forms for citing books may be slightly different than the forms used for citing articles in serial publications. In the same respect, the formats for citing graphics files or Web pages must take into account the usual citation practices of a discipline as well as the unique characteristics of these types of sources. Understanding the elements that, combined, constitute a citation and translating these elements for different types of sources will thereby allow researchers to cite existing sources as well as new types that may be necessary even when no explicit models are available.

2.1.5. The Principle of Transparency

This principle presumes that citation style should be as transparent, or as intuitive, as possible so that as many people as possible will be able to understand its codes. Different disciplines use different codes to represent the same information; however, within a discipline, the elements of citation are readily discernible without additional explanation. Scholars working in different fields come to recognize the various elements by their placement and formatting within a citation, allowing scholars to discern a given work's authority and currency quickly. For electronic sources, however, this kind of transparency may not always be possible.

2.2. RECONSIDERING THE PRINCIPLES OF CITATION ONLINE

Differences between the worlds of print and online publication require that we reconsider the principles of access, intellectual property, economy, standardization, and transparency. The principle of access, for instance, presents some intriguing challenges for citation in online documents. Attempting to ensure the verifiability of a writer's sources, while a worthwhile goal, involves problems of archiving, limited computer resources, and sometimes insufficient knowledge of how databases organize and present information that may preclude many authors from providing reliable annotation. For example, many online databases retrieve documents on the fly, creating the page in response to a request, so that the URL displayed in the browser's **location bar** may only exist momentarily. That is, the URL is really only a rendering of the search parameters and not an actual file address.

Even when the URL does provide direct access, lengthy addresses can be unwieldy and unforgiving, thus violating the principle of economy; that is, while an author may cut and paste the address into a bibliography, the URL may extend across many lines and require great care on the part of future researchers who may need to type in the address, character by character. An address such as the following can be quite tedious to type correctly:

> http://web19.epnet.com/citation.asp?tb=1&_ug=dbs=6+ln+en
> %2Dus+sid+90EBA77F%2D911A%2D4DBA%2DA2F7%2D
> 18197EDD5181%40sessionmgr3%2Dsessionmgr4+363E&_
> us=bs+rising++cost+cst+0%3B1%3B3+ds+rising++cost+ds
> tb+KS+hd+0+hs+%2D1+or+Date+ri+KAAACB2B0009385
> 4+sl+0+sm+KS+so+b+ss+SO+5DBB&cf=1&fn=1&rn=5

The principle of access would seem to require providing this information; however, in this case, providing the name of the database (EBSCO Host), along with any file numbers and publication information (e.g., author, title, etc.) of the referenced work, would still allow future researchers to access the file, even if the file should move. The following bibliographic citation provides the information necessary for a knowledgeable scholar to locate the article as well as providing important information that a scholar may use to evaluate the source (see chapter 1).

> Fine, Stuart. "The Rising Cost of Care: What's Really Driving Increased Spending." *AHA News* 30 Sep. 2002. 38.38: 4–5. *Health Source—Consumer Edition.* EBSCO Host. AN #7539510 (23 June 2003).

As with print-based publications, the principle of access maintains that a citation style should make access to cited online sources as efficient as possible. Using **hypertext** links to connect a quotation or a paraphrased idea to its original source if the original source is also located online would thus seem to best conform to the principles of access and transparency. If so, then bibliographic footnotes or endnotes would seem to be a waste of space and effort. That is, if readers can link directly to the original source, then providing notes would be a violation of the principle of economy. On the other hand, these principles might not seem as important when publishing online because the demands of electronic memory storage and distribution are typically insignificant compared with the financial and environmental costs of mass-produced ink-and-paper texts.

But what about the principle of standardization? Allowing automatic hypertextual links to replace standard bibliographic references may disrupt the standardized code on which academic readers have relied. Some readers of online work may not recognize or understand the nature of the hypertextual links to cited sources and may still look instead for bibliographic entries or, worse yet, not recognize that a quotation or paraphrase is being cited. Yet under the principle of transparency, hypertextual citation is nearly ideal in that it almost completely eliminates the need to decipher a code in order to access the original source. But, then again, could complete transparency begin to work against the principle of access and the overarching aim of knowledge building?

On the Web, documents tend to be published and vanish more quickly than do printed library books and academic journals. If an author relies solely on hypertextual links to refer to sources cited on the Web, what happens if the cited source is eventually moved—or removed altogether from the Web? Wouldn't a conventional bibliography provide a reasonable level of access while preventing some of the problems with a citation style that is too transparent? In other words, providing the elements of a typical citation—author, title, etc.—may help a committed scholar to relocate the information even if it moves or disappears. Thus, even though links can and should be used to facilitate access to online sources, this does not preclude the necessity of providing more conventional documentation.

Reconsidering the principle of intellectual property represents one of the most controversial and thorny issues surrounding online publication. Books, periodicals, films, audio recordings, and software programs may be fixed on a physical medium. But what happens when they move online? Current law stipulates that material protected by copyright must be fixed in some tangible medium. Are documents and journals on the World Wide Web fixed? Is the online world a tangible medium? When do electronic files become fixed? When they are saved to a hard drive or server? When they are printed out? What about files that are stored and read entirely online, such as electronic mail? And what about the inherent mutability of online writing? Even encouraging authors to retain copies (either electronic or paper) of sources they have referenced could violate current (or future) copyright laws. It therefore behooves authors to provide sufficient information about the sources on which they rely to ensure that credit is given where credit is due and to conform to the strictures of fair-use guidelines in addition to facilitating access to original materials.

Most Web documents are still being written and read by people raised and educated in a linear, print-based world. But online writing already means incorporating more than just words in our arrangements; we must now also consider the impact of links, graphics, animation, audio and video files, **flash** or **javascript** components, or database-driven compositions, as well as typographical elements such as fonts and white space. We can already include "smell" files (using scratch-and-sniff technologies) and touch (using **haptic** technologies) in our compositions. Still, the shift to a paperless age will not happen overnight, if at all, and although more and more of us are now beginning to write online, many of these works are still being written with print formats in mind, just as many texts originally intended for print are now being made available online. Moreover, screen technologies still do not always allow for comfortable reading of lengthy online works, such that many people still prefer to print out information. Formats for citing both electronic and traditional print sources therefore need to be readable in both print and electronic formats. And, as the Internet and other electronic sites continue to grow and change and we become more comfortable with reading and writing online, any guidelines we adopt will need to be flexible.

For now, the advice presented in this book will provide sufficient guidance to allow researchers to adequately acknowledge and cite most types of electronic and electronically accessed sources. Various discipline-specific style manuals give precise guidelines for citing other types of publications, including books, newspapers, journals, magazines, film clips, and more. When appropriate, authors should consult these manuals in addition to the present guide (see appendix D for a list of some of the more commonly used style manuals). For electronic sources, however, none of the major style manuals has presented adequate forms.

Columbia Online Style (COS) follows the logic upon which styles such as MLA (humanities) and APA (scientific) rely for print-based sources, but it applies this logic in a way that makes sense for online sources. As such, the *Columbia Guide to Online Style* is not meant to replace these styles but to supplement them, replacing only their often unwieldy and usually inadequate recommendations for citing electronic and electronically accessed sources. Moreover, the element approach used by COS offers a way to help researchers to provide adequate citation for new forms as they may emerge in the future.

2.3. UNDERSTANDING THE ELEMENT APPROACH TO ONLINE CITATION

Too many scholars neglect to include in their references important information about electronic and electronically published sources they use simply because they are unfamiliar with the terrain. That is, many people are still unsure what information they need to include and how to locate that information for online sources. As discussed in chapter 1, references should include sufficient information to allow readers to relocate a source as efficiently as possible as well as to allow them to evaluate the sources used in a given work by considering their authority, currency, and relevance. The various elements of a bibliographic entry work to facilitate both processes. Consider the following elements of citation for online sources.

2.3.1. Author Information

The first element for most citations is the name of the author or authors. The **ISO (International Standards Organization)** requires that the person or persons with "primary responsibility" for a referenced site be cited. Of course, the author is usually the person with primary responsibility. But, as with any kind of scholarship, those who contributed to the production of the work—including editors, compilers, translators, sponsors, and so forth—may need to be given credit as well.

2.3.1.1. Author's name. Humanities styles such as MLA require the full name of the author as listed on the title page or Web site (see chapter 3 for specific examples); scientific styles such as APA use the author's last name and initial(s) only (see chapter 4). Note that humanities style reverses the order of the first author or editor's name, but lists subsequent names in normal order (i.e., first name first), while the names of authors or editors in scientific style are all reversed, last name first, followed by initial(s). Scientific styles may also use the ampersand ("&") rather than spelling out the word "and" for multiple authors (e.g., Walker, J. R., & Taylor, T.) as in humanities styles.

An author's name is often listed at the beginning of an article or Web site, but sometimes it may be listed at the end—or not at all. You may need to check copyright statements as shown in Figure 2.1 or metatags (see chapter 1) for authorship information.

The TextArc site is generously hosted by Walrus Internet.
Site contents © 2002 by W. Bradford Paley, all rights reserved. TextArc technology is patent pending.

FIGURE 2.1 Check copyright statements for authorship information.

Source: http://textarc.org.

2.3.1.2. Aliases or fictitious names. Sometimes the only designation of an author may be an email address, as in figure 2.2. Only the **alias** or **login name**, "jwalker," not the author's full email address, is included in the bibliographic citation. In scientific style, personal correspondence of any kind, including email, is not usually included in the list of references; instead it is cited within the body of the text (see section 4.1). For both styles, other types of email messages, such as postings to a newsgroup or **listserv**, include the address of the listserv or discussion forum as well as the author's name or login identification (see also section 2.3.3.4).

Date: Fri, 17 Mar 2006 10:09:23 –0400 (EDT)

From: jwalker@georgiasouthern.edu

To: twtaylor@email.unc.edu

Subject: Electronic Mail Headers

FIGURE 2.2 An electronic mail header.

In some online synchronous (or real-time) communication sites (e.g., **chat rooms, MOOs, MUDs,** etc.), users may choose fictitious names or the database may randomly assign them "guest" names. To cite these conversations, use whatever author information is available. If you can determine the author's full name from an email **signature file** or header, for instance, then you may replace the author's login name or alias with the author's real name. Note that for synchronous or personal communications, however, you may need permission to quote participants, whether or not you use their real names.

2.3.1.3. Corporate or organizational authors. Instead of individual authors, some works are considered to be authored by an organization or group. Many news sites, for example, list the news service rather than an individual author's name (Associated Press or Reuters, for example). Similarly, corporate Web sites may contain information created by employees under an agreement known as "work for hire" where the corporation, rather than an individual, is considered the author. Names of organizations are capitalized as proper nouns in both styles. See chapters 3 and 4 for specific examples of how to cite articles with corporate or organizational authors and information from news services in humanities and scientific formats.

2.3.1.4. Editors, compilers, translators, etc. For sites that are compilations of the works of others or that pull together information from various sources, you may need to use the name of an editor, compiler, translator, moderator, or other person responsible for the information, as appropriate, including the abbreviated designation of responsibility after the person's name. For example, the site in figure 2.3 lists the name of the person who maintains the site rather than an author.

FIGURE 2.3 A Web site may list an editor, maintainer, or other person responsible for the site.

Source: http://homepages.law.asu.edu/~dkarjala/OpposingCopyrightExtension.

Include the designation of responsibility (e.g., maintainer, editor, etc.), abbreviated, after the name, separated by a comma in humanities style:

Karjala, Dennis S., maint.

Enclose the designation in parentheses in scientific style:

Karjala, D. S. (Maint.).

See appendix C for a list of recommended abbreviations. See chapter 3 for specific examples in humanities style; see chapter 4 for scientific styles.

2.3.1.5. No author. When no author or other person or organization is noted as responsible for the information on a site, begin the bibliographic entry with the title of the page or site, as appropriate. Include the date of publication, if known, after the title information for both styles. See specific examples in chapters 3 and 4. It is important to note, however, that authorship is an important element in determining the credibility of a source. Thus it is important to locate authorship information if possible, especially for sources on which your own arguments depend (see also section 2.3.1.8 for information on sponsorship). Check copyright statements, metatags, or links on the site, or try moving "up" the URL to determine authorship information. For more information, see chapter 1.

2.3.2. Title of Page or Article and File Names

Determining title information for electronic documents and files is often difficult. For example, in figure 2.4 the author has included a title on the page, but the hypertext header lists another title, as shown in the title bar at the top of the browser. (For more information on titles in hypertext documents, see also part 2).

For most citation purposes, use the title on the page itself, if available, as provided by the author. When the Web page or article does not include a title, check the **title bar**. Be careful, however; the title-bar information may refer to the page, to the site, to a sponsoring organization, or even to an **Internet service provider** who offers Web publishing space but is not responsible in any way for the information presented. Your determination of title information, then, may need to rely on your detective work (see chapter 1) as well as on your own critical reading—and critical thinking—skills. For academic documents on the World Wide Web, part 2 of this book outlines suggestions to help standardize title information. Authors should follow these guidelines when feasible. One suggestion we have made in this book is to use the file names to

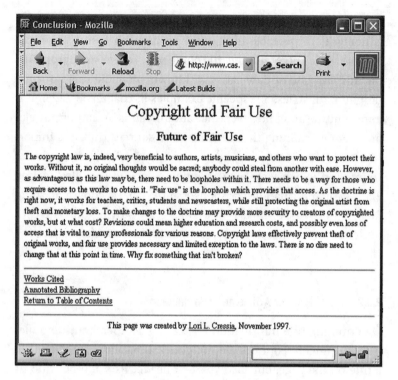

FIGURE 2.4 A hypertext page with titles and headers.

Source: http://www.cas.usf.edu/english/walker/courses/fall97/concl.html.

cite information when no title information is available (see sec. 2.3.2.2.). Other solutions may become apparent as the electronic world continues to evolve.

2.3.2.1. Article and Web page titles. Enclose the titles of online articles and Web pages in quotation marks for humanities style, capitalizing the first word and all major words. In scientific style, capitalize only the first word, proper nouns, and the first word after a colon in the title, if applicable; do not use quotation marks. Follow with publication information, e.g., the title of the online newspaper, journal, or Web site, in italics, including the date of publication, volume or issue numbers (if applicable), and location (usually the URL). Titles are usually located at the top (or beginning) of a Web page or article, often in a different font (larger or boldfaced, for example). You may also need to check title bars (see figure 2.4), metatags (see chapter 1), or citation information that the author may include, as does the page illustrated in figure 2.5.

Publication Information: Childers, Pamela B. (2003). WAC/CAC in secondary schools: Learning from Our Colleagues. *Academic.Writing,* http://wac.colostate.edu/aw/secondary/column7.htm
Publication Date: June 3, 2003

FIGURE 2.5   Publication information included on a Web page.
Source: Academic.Writing, http://wac.colostate.edu/aw/secondary/column7.htm.

2.3.2.2. Untitled files. Untitled files (including most personal home pages) are often treated the same as unpublished works: the file name is not enclosed in quotation marks or italicized. A description of the file may be included in the bibliographic citation as well. An untitled home page, for example, may include the designation "Home Page" after the author information in humanities style:

Humanities Style

Walker, Janice R. Home Page. 5 Apr. 2003. http://www.GeorgiaSouthern.edu/~jwalker (18 Mar. 2006).

In scientific style, place the date of publication immediately following the name of the author:

Scientific Style

Walker, J. R. (2003, April 5). Home page. http://www.GeorgiaSouthern.edu/~jwalker/ (18 Mar. 2006).

For both humanities and scientific styles, a home page that is not part of a larger site may be treated either as an article (see section 2.3.2.1) or as an unpublished work, depending on the content. Corporate and organizational home pages without titles are cited similarly (see chapters 3 and 4).

For graphics or other electronic files with no title, references may include the file name (e.g., index.html), using the exact capitalization and formatting as indicated in the URL or location bar. Do not italicize or enclose file names in quotation marks. Some styles also include an indication of the type of file, usually enclosed in square brackets and immediately following the title or file name, for example,

eel.gif [graphic file].

The file extension (e.g., ".gif") already indicates the file type, of course, so the addition of the descriptor may be redundant and certainly violates the principle of economy. However, since many people may not recognize various file extensions, especially because file extensions in some operating systems are suppressed and since file extensions may certainly change in the future, adding a description of the file type can aid in ensuring conformance to the first principle of citation, that of access.

When no author or other person or organization is listed, the bibliographic entry in both styles will begin with the title or file name. See examples in chapters 3 (humanities style) and 4 (scientific style).

2.3.2.3. Parts of works. Words that designate specific parts of a work (e.g., preface or abstract), are formatted similarly to home pages, that is, they are not enclosed in quotation marks or italicized. Humanities style includes the designation or description (e.g., abstract) immediately preceding the title. Scientific style includes the designation or description immediately after the title, enclosed in square brackets and prior to the end punctuation. It is important to note when you are citing an abstract or summary of an article, such as is often the case with information presented in online databases, rather than the full text of an article. Some databases offer access to both abstracts and full text; some offer only an abstract. If possible, of course, you will want to consult the full article (see also chapter 1). For specific examples, see chapter 3 for humanities styles; see chapter 4 for scientific styles.

2.3.3. Titles of Web Sites, Online Books, Journals, and Other Complete Works

Many Internet documents and files are brief, and it is often difficult or impossible to ascertain if they are part of a larger body of work or can be considered to be independently published. If you know that a given Web page is part of a larger work published online, then you should designate it as such (see section 2.3.2.1). Cite an entire Web site, book, or journal published online or on CD-ROM or through another electronic medium just as you would a similar print publication, italicizing the title and including any volume, issue, or page numbers, if applicable.

Do not underline book, magazine, or journal titles; underlining indicates text that should be italicized in final printed publications and is a carryover from the old days of typewriters and old-fashioned fonts (such as Courier) which made it difficult for editors (and teachers) to determine if titles were formatted correctly by authors. Nowadays, however, readers familiar with the conventions of many Internet browsers often expect underlined text to represent a hyperlink. Use italics to format these titles; underlining should only be used to format book and journal titles when required by editors or teachers, or, instead, you may need to mark up your manuscript using **document-type definitions** (DTDs) such as **XML** or another markup language (see part 2).

A document may be published in a stand-alone version as well as within a larger work, such as an online journal. The file may or may not use the same title at both addresses, or one version may change while the other remains static. Graphics, audio, video, and other types of multimedia files may not provide any title information at all. Names given to objects in role-playing games and synchronous communication sites such as MOOs and MUDs or in database-driven essays pose similar dilemmas, as object names or aliases may change at any time although the object number remains the same—at least until the object is recycled. Check the title bar, any "About this Site" links, copyright statements, or metatags; try moving "up" the URL if necessary to determine information about the site (see also chapter 1). Ultimately, however, determining the format to use to present information that does not fit neatly into any category may depend on your own critical thinking skills and understanding of the needs and expectations of your readers.

2.3.3.1. Web sites. A Web site consists of multiple articles and files or Web pages. Cite an entire Web site title as you would a book, italicizing the title and providing the URL for the opening or main page of the site. Check title bars, links, or other information that may be useful in helping you to determine title information (see also chapter 1). To cite specific pages within a site, see section 2.3.2.

2.3.3.2. Online books. To cite a book published on the World Wide Web, include the author's name; the book title, in italics; the date of publication (if known); the protocol and address; and the date accessed. Print publication information should be included if available, followed by the electronic publication information. See chapters 3 and 4 for specific examples. Works that have been previously published online may include original online publication information as well. Some of these sites may be "**mirrors**," that is, they have copied information published at another domain; some may be discrete editions. The information at the original site may have changed, however, without notification to the mirror sites. Other works may be published on a personal site as well as in an online journal. If possible, consult the original or published source (print or electronic, as applicable) since the published version will usually be considered the more authoritative one. At any rate, make sure to cite the actual edition used (see section 2.3.4).

2.3.3.3. Online journals. An online journal generally includes articles by various authors. Italicize titles of online journals or other periodicals, capitalizing the first word and all major words in both humanities and scientific styles (journal titles are treated as proper nouns in scientific styles). The volume and issue number for a journal are not italicized in humanities style, and no punctuation separates the journal title and the volume number (see section 3.2.1.8). Journal titles in scientific style follow the same rules of formatting (i.e., italics) and capitalization as humanities style; however, a comma follows the journal title, the volume number is italicized, and the issue number is enclosed in parentheses but not italicized (see section 4.2.1.8).

2.3.3.4. Other complete works. As noted previously, titles of online books, journals, and similar works should be italicized. You should also italicize the name of online sites such as MOOs and MUDs, electronic databases, Internet Service Provider (ISP) sites such as *America Online* (see also section 2.3.5.2), electronic mailing lists, software packages, or other sites that collect and present information or the works of multiple authors.

2.3.4. Edition or Version Information, If Applicable

An edition of a book or article may represent a substantial revision from the original or previously published version. Sometimes, however, an edition represents merely a change in medium, for example, a hardcover edition versus a paperback one. At any rate, editions are important to note in references to sources because even relatively minor changes can sometimes have a profound effect. Moreover, especially for scholarly work, some editions are considered more authoritative than others. New editions sometimes correct errors in older editions, include additional material, or add explications not found in older editions. An edition may be incomplete—an abridged edition, for example—or offer updates or emendations. In order for future researchers to verify the accuracy and reliability of an author's work, the exact edition used must be noted.

Electronic sources, even those that are supposedly exact replications of print sources, constitute unique editions. Converting print-based files to electronic ones may introduce errors, or editors may correct errors in the original when converting files. Citations of electronic files created from print-based sources should include both print publication information and electronic publication information.

Files that are created explicitly for electronic publication, including Web pages, **e-books**, and online articles, may also be corrected or changed with no notice (see also section 2.3.6). The date the file is accessed by the researcher is thus important to note, since the only surety that the researcher may offer is that the information was there on the date he or she last accessed it. In effect, then, the access date designates the unique "edition" of what may be a volatile source (see section 2.3.9).

If a file includes edition information, such as version numbers; publication, revision, or modification dates; etc., as does the site in figure 2.6, this information should be included in the reference. Future researchers, then, can attempt to locate the exact edition or version to determine its credibility or to extract additional information as needed. For specific examples, see chapters 3 (humanities) and 4 (scientific).

W3C Recommendation

XForms 1.0 (Second Edition)

W3C Recommendation 14 March 2006

This version:
 http://www.w3.org/TR/2006/REC-xforms-20060314/
Latest version:
 http://www.w3.org/TR/xforms/
Previous version:
 http://www.w3.org/TR/2003/REC-xforms-20031014/
Editors:
 John M. Boyer, IBM
 David Landwehr, Novell
 Roland Merrick, IBM
 T. V. Raman, Google
 Micah Dubinko, Cardiff Software - (First Edition)
 Leigh L. Klotz, Jr., Xerox Corporation - (First Edition)

Please refer to the errata for this document, which may include normative corrections.

This document is also available in these non-normative formats: single HTML file diff-marked HTML Zip archive .

The English version of this specification is the only normative version. Non-normative translations may also be available.

Copyright © 2006 W3C® (MIT, ERCIM, Keio), All Rights Reserved. W3C liability, trademark and document use rules apply.

FIGURE 2.6 Noting version or edition information.
Source: http://www.w3.org/TR/2006/REC-xforms-20060314.

2.3.5. Publication Information

Traditional citation formats include the city of publication and the publisher's name. This information allows users to locate a given source more easily: if it is not available in the library, we may contact the publisher. We can also be assured we are using the same source as that referenced. Additionally, the name of the press has often been a means of determining the reliability of a given work for academic purposes, with university presses generally considered to be better sources than more popular ones (see also chapter 1). Publication information for electronic and electronically accessed sources should be included when available. For many World Wide Web documents and files, however, the URL provides the only available publication information.

2.3.5.1. Internet sources. The first part of the URL designates the protocol. This is followed by the domain name, which indicates the server where the work is published, plus any directories and subdirectories, and, finally, the file name. Thus the URL provides the information necessary to access a source and replaces the usual publication information required for citations of print publications. The domain name, like a publisher's imprint, may help a reader locate a particular source; if a work is no longer available at a given URL, it may be possible to contact the Web master for the domain and locate the author or file. If a file is located within the same domain as a given URL, even if the file name or directory name has changed, we can also be fairly sure we are looking at the same file as that referenced and not at a mirror site or some other work with the same title. Domain names may also help somewhat to determine the reliability of an online source. Whether a file is located on an educational server or a commercial server may provide some sense of its reliability. However, as for print sources, the ultimate test of reliability is not who published it but the text itself and the critical reading and thinking skills of those who rely on it. For more information on evaluating sources, see chapter 1.

Publication information for online sources includes the protocol and address or the name of the information provider (e.g., *America Online*) or database (see section 2.3.5.2), plus any commands, search terms, or file numbers useful in locating the source (see section 2.3.8). The URL in the citation for an article may lead to the main page of the journal or site in order to allow researchers to determine the credibility of the source and to avoid long and unwieldy addresses, but a direct link to the Web page or article could also be used. Be careful, however; often, online journals and sites present information within frames. The URL shown in the location bar will then lead to the main page of the site rather than directly to the article, or it may even lead to pages outside the journal or Web site, even though the pages appear within the same frame. For instance, in figure 2.7, the opening page for the

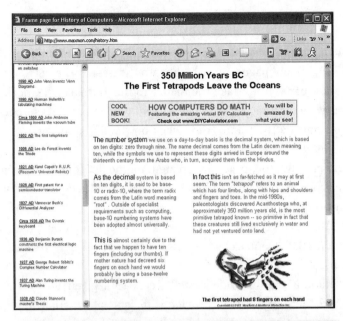

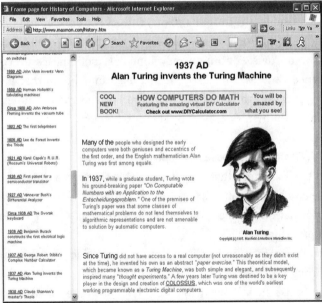

FIGURE 2.7 The URL in the location bar remains the same for pages opened inside frames, even though the page is at a different location.

Source: http://www.maxmon.com/history.htm.

online journal *Academic.Writing* appears inside the frame for the personal home page from which it was accessed. The URL in the location bar will not take the reader to the journal site. Check to ensure the accuracy of your citations by opening the referenced pages outside the frame (right click on the link and open it in a new window).

Sometimes, too, pages are created "on the fly" (that is, information is retrieved from a searchable database only on demand). URLs may only represent the temporary search results and not be useful for reaccessing the specific combination of information cited (see section 2.3.8). Double check URLs in your bibliography; try accessing them in a new browser window to make sure they work.

Citations may provide direct access to a given file within a site, or they may instead provide sufficient information to allow researchers to access the cited information from the main page of the site, usually the author's name, title of the article, and date of publication and/or volume and issue numbers for online magazines or journals. For online encyclopedias, dictionaries, and other reference sources, the search terms used may be all that is necessary to locate the cited information. For specific examples, see chapter 3 (humanities style) or chapter 4 (scientific style).

2.3.5.2. Electronic databases and information services. Electronic databases such as those that may be available through a library's Web site and reference sources (e.g., an encyclopedia) accessed through an information service provider such as *America Online* will often list a publisher as well.

Databases may be published online, available by subscription or through a library's Web portal. Web pages, articles, and even entire books may be available through an online database or an information provider. A URL will not usually provide access to this information. However, users may arrange to obtain the information by accessing the database through their own library's Web portal or by subscribing to the information service. Include the name of the database or the name of the information service (e.g., *America Online*), in italics, followed by the name of the database publisher (if applicable) and any file numbers or search terms necessary to locate the original information. Be careful, however; databases may provide access to the full text of the article or merely to an abstract of the article (see section 2.3.2.3). For examples of other types of sources, see chapters 3 and 4.

2.3.5.3. Publications on fixed media. In citations of electronic sources published on fixed media, such as CD-ROM, diskettes, or magnetic tape, include the city of publication and the name of the publisher, if known, along with the date of publication or release and any file numbers, keywords, or search-path information necessary to locate the information being cited (see also section 2.3.5.2). Citations of sources published on fixed media, like their print counterparts, need not include the date of access. For these sources, the version number (see section 2.3.4) or publication date (see section 2.3.6) is sufficient.

An important feature of electronic files is that they are readily transferable from one medium to another: files may be downloaded from their online homes and saved to disks; CD-ROM titles may be installed on a user's hard drive; and most formats may be printed out. For this reason, identifying the publication medium in the bibliographic reference may be meaningless. It certainly violates the principle of economy in that the protocol or publication information is usually sufficient to locate the source. Even designating a specific software-publication medium such as CD-ROM is problematic. Some software is available on either diskette or CD-ROM or may be downloaded from an Internet site with no change in the content of the software package itself. There are important differences, however, between one version of the software and the next; thus, indicating the version number and date of publication is key to pointing the reader to a specific edition.

2.3.6. Date of Publication, Last Revision, or Modification

Publication, revision, or modification dates, if known, should be included in the citation (see also section 2.3.4). In humanities style, place the document date and/or the date of last revision or modification after the title in international date format (i.e., day, month, and year), using the three-letter abbreviation for months of more than four letters (see appendix D). In scientific style, the document date is enclosed in parentheses and placed after the author's name; the month is not abbreviated in scientific style. Date formats vary for different types of sources. See specific examples in chapters 3 and 4.

2.3.7. Page Numbers or Location

Some people still believe that a publication of one or two pages is not a reliable source of information for academic works. On the Web, however, a given file is always one page, regardless of its length. Pagination is thus an element of print publication that has little or no meaning in electronic documents and files. It is handy for locating a specific part of a text, however, and to replace it many software packages offer search or find features. Authors may also choose to embed page **anchors**, section numbers, or other navigational features within electronic files. In some instances, it may even be possible for authors to link to specific parts of other works, even those whose authors have not provided the means for doing so.

Screens, printer dependency, monitor capability, and software all affect "page" or "screen" representations. Thus, unless an author has included page numbers in an electronic file, these representations cannot be used effectively in citations. In any case, pagination is an artifact of print culture and unnecessary in citations for most electronic sources, which can usually be searched for keywords and phrases using search or find protocols in most word-processing software and Internet browsers. What cannot be omitted, however, is information to allow readers to locate the source itself.

Articles that have been published previously in print, PDF (Portable Document Format) files, and other files that have designated pagination should include page numbers in references just as for print sources. List the page numbers for the entire article in bibliographic references along with the print publication information if known. Page numbers will also be included in parenthetic notes in the text itself if the version you consult online includes page numbers (such as will usually be the case for PDF files). For electronic sources that do not designate page numbers, however, you may need to repeat the author's name in the parenthetic note in order to be sure that your readers will know you are citing a source, or you may decide to include the designation "n.p." (for "not paginated") instead. For Web sites or other types of sources that consist of multiple discrete files, you may give the file name for reference to the location of the information or quotation (e.g., index.html for information that appears on the opening page of a site). See chapters 3 and 4 for more information on in-text notations.

2.3.8. Sponsoring Organizations, Conferences, and Series Names

Corporate authorship is not the same as sponsorship (see section 2.3.1.3). A corporate or organizational sponsor may be noted after the title information. Likewise, papers that have been presented at professional conferences include the name of the conference, its location, and the date of presentation following the title information. Books or works that are part of a series include the title of the book in italics in addition to the title of the series (not italicized) and, if applicable, the name(s) of the series editor(s). See specific examples in chapters 3 and 4.

2.3.9. File Numbers, Search Terms, or Other Information

Many online databases use various document or file numbers that can help to identify a specific document. Identify accession numbers (AN), international standard serial numbers (ISSN), digital object identifiers (DOI), or other document or file numbers to facilitate access and identification of sources.

For most online or electronic encyclopedia, dictionary, or thesaurus entries, the search terms constitute the title of the document or file. For example, to cite an unsigned article on "gastroenterology," begin with the term, capitalized as for article titles. In humanities style, enclose the term in quotation marks. If the article or reference entry lists an author, begin with the author's name followed by the term, formatted as above (see sections 3.2.2 and 4.2.2)

For some online sites, direct access to a file may not be possible or desirable. For searchable online databases that do not allow ready access to a file by author, title, or other publication information, include the search terms used to locate the information following the URL of the main search page for the site or the name of the database or information service. Information providers such as *America Online*, for example, often allow access to information using keywords that should be included in the citation following the name of the service. Alternatively, you may need to provide the path you followed from a main page or site, identifying each link along the way. Separate links with a forward slash mark ("/"). See chapter 3 (humanities style) or chapter 4 (scientific style) for specific examples.

2.3.10. Date of Access

Because many Web sites do not include publication or revision dates, the date of access may often be the only way to designate what amounts to the edition of the work in **cyberspace**, especially since an author may have altered an online document without changing its dates. Thus, the access date identifies the unique edition of the work that a writer has referenced. It is placed in parentheses at the end of the citation, after the Internet address in day-month-year format (e.g., "8 July 2003"). The parentheses surrounding the address are used because the date is not part of the file or article itself but is included for information purposes only. For fixed media, such as works published on CD-ROM, the date of access is unnecessary since the information published in a specific version of a software package will remain the same regardless of when it is accessed (see also section 2.3.5.3).

Chapters 3 and 4 provide specific information and examples of in-text and bibliographic forms for a variety of commonly used types of electronic and electronically accessed sources in humanities-based (e.g., MLA) and scientific-based (e.g., APA) styles. For information on other commonly used formats such as footnotes and endnotes (e.g., Chicago) or Council of Science Editors styles, see appendix D.

3

CITING ELECTRONIC SOURCES IN THE HUMANITIES

The primary elements of a bibliographic reference are the same for most styles of documentation, although the order in which they are presented may vary. This chapter gives examples of citations according to a humanities style based on MLA criteria but modified to make sense for electronic and electronically accessed sources. For a scientific style based on APA criteria, see chapter 4. For other styles, you can translate the various required elements (e.g., author's name(s), titles, dates, etc.) following the models in these two chapters. See also appendix D for some examples of styles using footnotes and endnotes.

Citations usually involve two steps: first, a note in the text acknowledges information, words, or ideas from other sources, either directly or parenthetically; and second, a bibliographic entry in a list of works cited provides full publication information for all sources cited in the text. Bibliographic citations usually include acknowledgment of the author, the title of the article or file, the title of the complete work, publication information (usually including place of publication and publisher's name, or the electronic address, and the date of publication), and the page number(s) of the article or chapter, if applicable. Parenthetic references in the body of the text usually include the author's last name and the page number (if applicable) for the cited passage. The page number identifies the exact location within a document where a specific reference can be found, while the author's last name points to the full citation in the list of works cited. In-text notes thus help to support an author's assertions by pointing to information about the credentials of the sources upon which the author has relied (see also chapter 1).

Citing print resources is not always straightforward, of course, but for the most part, the necessary information is readily available. For electronic sources, some elements may be missing or must be translated into elements that make sense in a new era of publishing (see chapter 2). When in doubt, it is better to give too much information than too little. For print-based sources, follow the guidelines included in the *MLA Handbook for Writers of Research Papers*. The models provided in this chapter are designed to work *with* MLA guidelines for citing print sources, replacing the often unwieldy and incomplete guidelines for electronic and electronically accessed sources in ways that make sense for a new era of publishing.

3.1. DOCUMENTING SOURCES IN THE TEXT

As noted earlier, parenthetical or in-text references to print publications usually include the author's last name and the page number of the reference. Following the principle of economy, subsequent references to the same work usually include only a page number until another in-text reference intervenes, as illustrated in figure 3.1.

Brown 7

The elements of citation for print-based sources must be translated in ways that make sense for electronic publications **(Walker and Taylor 33)**. That is, such features as page numbering may not make sense online **(35)**. Other major styles, however, still seem to support the notion that features such as pagination—or at least paragraph numbering—are necessary even for online publication. Thus the Modern Language Association, for instance, suggests that "numbering paragraphs is becoming common in electronic publications" **(Gibaldi 138)**, even though most software used to access and read electronically published work readily allows for users to search for specific instances of text **(Walker and Taylor 35)**.

FIGURE 3.1 Citing references in parenthetical notes in humanities style.

3.1.1. Citations Without Page Numbers

For electronic sources, unless the author has specifically designated "page" numbers (or other identifiers such as paragraph or section numbers) within the document or file, pagination simply does not exist (see also section 2.3.7). Thus, in-text references for electronic sources usually include only the author's last name. For example,

> One fact that cannot be denied is that "We live in an age in which rapid change is certain" (Ambrose).

Subsequent references may then need to repeat the author's last name in order to document any borrowings. If there are multiple references to the same source within a paragraph, reserve the parenthetical material for the end of the paragraph. Whenever possible, you should incorporate references into the text itself to avoid awkwardness.

When the author's name is included in the text, omit the parenthetical reference:

> According to Stephen Ambrose, the real technological revolution began in the nineteenth century, not the twentieth.

The entry in the list of works cited for this reference would begin with the author's last name (Ambrose) followed by the title and publication information. Thus the in-text reference points the reader to the bibliographic entry. Identifying your sources in the body of your text also helps to lend credibility to your arguments which rely on these sources. For example:

> According to Stephen Ambrose, former professor emeritus of history at the University of New Orleans and best-selling author, . . .

Identify details of studies and other sources of statistics and facts in a similar manner:

> According to a 2003 study sponsored by the Pew Internet and American Life Project, as many as thirty-five million adults have downloaded music files from the Internet (Madden and Lenhart).

The authors of the report in the preceding example are identified in a parenthetic note that points to the bibliographic entry beginning with their names. Use parenthetical references to identify the authors of a study when they are not named in the text, the source of noncontroversial statistical information, the page number or specific location of information in files, or other types of information that does not need to be supported in the text (see also chapter 1 on locating and evaluating information).

In place of page numbers, you may use file names in parenthetic notes to denote specific "pages" (e.g., specific files) within a larger Web site. For example:

> In a forum on "The Role of Technology in WAC/CAC Programs," Michael Day, a writing program administrator at Northern Illinois University, recommends that "beyond incorporating networked technologies for interaction in WAC/CAC programs, we need to adopt, adapt, or develop assessment procedures for the technologies we use" (Palmquist day_closing.htm).

The full bibliographic reference for this citation would point to the beginning page of the journal or article, moderated by Michael Palmquist. Note that no punctuation separates the file name from the author's or moderator's last name, just as no punctuation separates an author's name and page number in traditional print citations.

3.1.2. Citations with Section, Paragraph, or Line Numbers

List section, paragraph, or line numbers at the conclusion of the citation, separated by commas, if they are included in the original file:

> One important reason for the move to electronic writing is that "it is becoming very much cheaper to store information in electronic form and comparatively more expensive to store it as paper" (Goodwin, sec. 1.1).

If the author's name is cited in the text, list only the paragraph, section, or line number in parentheses at the end of the reference:

> John E. Goodwin notes that one reason for the move to electronic writing is that it is cheaper (sec. 1.1).

Some styles suggest counting paragraphs for Web articles in order to designate the specific location of information in the source; however, this could be cumbersome as well as unnecessary (thus violating the principle of economy) since most electronically published sources are easily searched using the search or find features in word processors, Web browsers, or other software. Check your references to ensure that readers can locate the cited information; provide whatever information may be necessary to aid a reasonably knowledgeable reader to the source.

3.1.3. Citing Multiple Works by the Same Author

For multiple works by the same author, include the author's last name, followed by a comma and a shortened version of the title, italicized or enclosed in quotation marks as applicable (see chapter 2), including the exact page number of the reference if known. For example:

> The author is best known, perhaps, for his colorful depictions of life on the Mississippi River and use of dialect: "Whar is you? Dog my cats ef I didn' hear sumf'n," says Jim, the slave (Twain, *Huckleberry Finn*). The use of dialect is evident in other works as well, reaching across the globe and back across the centuries, to King Arthur's Court, using key words and phrases such as "Marry" and "Prithee" to lend credibility to an incredible story (Twain, *Connecticut Yankee*).

Again, if any of this information is mentioned in the text, there is no need to provide it within parentheses as well:

Mark Twain is best known, perhaps for his colorful depictions of life on the Mississippi River and use of dialect: "Whar is you? Dog my cats ef I didn' hear sumf'n," says Jim, the slave, in Twain's *Huckleberry Finn.*

In the list of works cited, replace second and subsequent listings of the author's name with three dashes. Alphabetize the works by the first major word of the title.

Twain, Mark. *The Adventures of Huckleberry Finn.* New York: Harper and Brothers, 1884. *Electronic Text Center.* U of Virginia Library. http://etext.lib.virginia.edu/toc/modeng/ public/Twa2Huc.html (18 Mar. 2006).

———. *A Connecticut Yankee in King Arthur's Court.* New York: Harper and Brothers, 1889. *Electronic Text Center.* U of Virginia Library. http://etext.lib.virginia.edu/toc/modeng/ public/TwaYank.html (8 Mar. 2006).

3.1.4. Citations with Corporate or Organizational Author

When no individual is named as the author or responsible party (e.g., a moderator, editor, or other person or persons with responsibility for the information contained in an article or Web site), cite the name of the corporation, organization, or news service in the body of the text or in the parenthetic note.

The National Council of Teachers of English (NCTE) in their position statement on writing assessment notes that . . .

Scientists predict that the Hubble space telescope could come careening back to earth by the year 2013 unless action is taken soon (Reuters).

3.1.5. Citations with No Known Author

For in-text citations when no author or organization is listed, use the document title or a shortened version of the title, enclosed in quotation marks or italicized as appropriate, instead of the author's name:

> ("Copyright Resources")

> (*CNN.Com*)

3.1.6. Citations with No Author or Title

Avoid awkward citations, especially for articles without individual authors and titles, by including the reference in the text rather than a parenthetic note.

> According to the Microsoft Web site . . .

The bibliographic entry for this reference would begin with the name of the corporate author (e.g., Microsoft).

For citations with no author or title, use the file name in the parenthetic note when it begins the bibliographic entry (see also section 3.2.1.6).

> The comet's tail appears as a streak of light (01K5_030706_gs1.jpg).

3.1.7. Citations of Multiple Works with the Same Titles and No Author

When you have multiple anonymous works with the same title, in addition to including the title in the parenthetic note, you may need to include additional information to allow your readers to differentiate between sources. If the page or article is part of a larger site, include the site title after the page title.

According to some accounts, John Donne was a "nice guy" ("John Donne," *Incompetech*). His life, however, was not an easy one ("John Donne," *England Online*).

When there is no site title, or when site titles are the same, include the date of publication or last modification, the file or domain name, or even the full URL, if necessary, so that your reader will be able to ascertain to which entry in the list of works cited your parenthetic note refers.

Because he was a Catholic, he was not allowed to receive the degree he earned from Oxford and Cambridge ("John Donne," authors_donne.htm) even though he later betrayed his faith ("John Donne," Donne.html).

3.1.8. Citations of Graphics, Audio, or Video Files

The format for citing graphics, audio, or video files, including **podcasts**, for example, in the body of the text depends a great deal on how they are being used. If you are referencing a file published online, include the artist's or creator's name, if known and if not included in the body of the text, or the file name (see section 3.1.6) in the parenthetic note.

The light curve for the comet Encke, for example . . . (Morris).

The tail of the comet Encke appears . . . (encke.93oct24.gif).

Files that you have downloaded or copied from other sources to include in your own paper or Web site need to include the source information as well. You may include a "source" line for images or files as illustrated in figure 3.2.

Alternatively, you may include a "credits" page or list of figures.

Fig 1. Photograph of the Supreme Court (Source:
http://www.whitehouse.gov/government/images/supremecourt.jpg)

FIGURE 3.2 Cite the source of individual graphics or pictures in humanities style.

For example, a Web page with multiple images from a free online graphics site may include a note giving credit:

> All images on this page courtesy of FreeGraphics.Org, http://www.freegraphics.org.

Web pages may also include **mouseovers** with credit lines, and files may be linked to online sources. But be careful—mouseovers and links will not be sufficient if the page is printed out; mouseovers may not work in different browsers or with different settings; and even links will not work if the original source moves or even disappears.

Unfortunately, as easy as it is to download or scan in graphics or other files, citation is not enough to conform to intellectual property laws. Before using these types of files, you may need to obtain permission. Government sources are considered owned by the general public, unless otherwise noted, and many sites offer free graphics files. But downloading audio, video, or graphics or scanning in images from print sources without permission can result in legal penalties, even if the source is cited.

It is usually not necessary to include multimedia files in the list of works cited unless you are referring to them in your text. That is, if graphics or other types of multimedia files are used merely for decorative purposes, then the source information in the label or credits is sufficient (see also section 3.2.1.22).

3.1.9. Citations of Personal Communications

Personal communications, such as personal email or other written correspondence, chat room, telephone, or even face-to-face conversations need to be noted in the text as well. Reference conversations directly by describing them in the body of your text, or include them in a parenthetic note.

> In a conversation with participants at the Netoric Project's *Tuesday Café*, a weekly meeting of academics in computers and writing at Connections MOO, Tari Fanderclai argued that . . .

> The much-heralded anonymity of cyberspace may soon be a thing of the past, if it ever really existed at all. A frequent lament is that "Everyone wants to see my picture online before they'll even chat with me nowadays" (mbrown2137).

3.1.10. Citations of Legal and Biblical References

Citing legal information may be complex. In general, include information about familiar legal statutes and cases in parenthetic notes, including the year of the statute or case when appropriate, as well as any other pertinent information.

> The law stipulates that states may allow abortions to be performed only by licensed physicians (Roe v. Wade, 410 US 113, Supreme Ct. of the US. 22 Jan. 1973, 165).

> Congress was granted the power to impose taxes (US Const., art. 1, sec. 8).

Do not italicize the titles of legal codes, statutes, or cases, or enclose them in quotation marks. References to well-known laws and documents, such as the U.S. Constitution or the U.S. Code, do not need to be included in the list of works cited. For more information on citing legal sources, see *The Blue Book: A Uniform System of Citation* (Harvard Law Review) or more general works such as *The Chicago Manual of Style*. The Libraries at Arizona State University offer a wonderful online guide to citing government documents following MLA and APA styles at http://www.asu.edu/lib/hayden/govdocs/docscite/docscite.htm.

Biblical and other sacred references, like legal references, do not need to be included in the list of works cited, unless you are referencing a specific edition or translation, but should be acknowledged in the text or in an in-text note. In general, do not enclose the titles of books of the Bible or other sacred writings in quotation marks and do not italicize. You may abbreviate references to well known titles in the parenthetic note.

David appointed keepers of the sacred ark from among the tribe of Levites (1 Chron. 16.4).

3.2. PREPARING THE BIBLIOGRAPHIC MATERIAL

When preparing documents for print, the list of works cited should begin on a separate page immediately following the text. The pages should be numbered sequentially and double-spaced throughout. Use a **hanging indent** when listing entries, so that the first line of each entry is flush with the left-hand margin and with second and subsequent lines of each entry indented five spaces or one-half inch. Do *not* use the space bar or tab key to indent lines; instead, use the hanging indent feature in your word processor, or set the left margin so that run-over lines are indented automatically. Final published manuscripts are usually set single-spaced throughout.

For hypertext documents, the list of works cited may be a separate "page" or file, or it may be placed at the end of a document. Because hypertexts are, in effect, published manuscripts, that is, they are made publicly available on the World Wide Web, do *not* double space the entries or use the hanging indent feature. Instead, you may want to single space the entire manuscript, including entries in the list of works cited, using the paragraph break code ("<p>") to double-space between them, or you may want to use a bulleted or unordered list to format them. For more information on preparing documents in print and electronic format, see part 2.

For both print and electronic documents, titles of complete works should be italicized rather than underlined because, as noted in chapter 2, underlining indicates text that should be italicized. Hypertext links in electronic files may be automatically formatted by your word processor or Web page editor, usually with a different font size or color and underlining, which most readers these days will readily recognize as a link. For printed papers, you may choose to remove the formatting or you may leave it as is unless your teacher, editor, or publisher requires you to format linked text a certain way (see part 2 for more information). For projects to be read electronically (e.g., created with a word processor and transmitted electronically or hypertexts published on the World Wide Web), URLs in the bibliographic entries should be formatted as links, in conformance with the principles of transparency and access (see chapter 2). Do not introduce line breaks into URLs; allow your word processor to automatically wrap the lines, even if it introduces some awkward-looking line breaks, again unless you are required to do otherwise.

The basic format for citing electronic sources in humanities style is:

Author's Last Name, First Name. "Title of Document." *Title of Complete Work.* Version or Edition. Document date or date of last revision or modification. Protocol and address or *Name of database* and Publisher (access path, directories, keywords, or file numbers [if applicable]) (date of access).

When information is not available, obviously you cannot include it, but give as much information as you can. See also chapters 1 and 2 for more on locating bibliographical information.

Although this basic model can help you determine the information necessary to cite most electronic or electronically accessed files, there are so many variations that it is not possible for one model to work for all of them. The rest of this chapter provides models for many of the most commonly used—and some of the most troublesome—types of electronic sources, based on years of questions from students, researchers, and editors, organized by the type of information source. Also see chapter 2 for more information about the elements included in bibliographic citations. For other types of sources, you may need to refer to chapter 2 to help you translate the required elements of citation.

3.2.1. Web Pages or Sites

The World Wide Web has made finding information on the Internet quicker and easier and is quickly gaining acceptance as a site for research and publication. Point-and-click browsers such as Netscape *Navigator*, Microsoft *Internet Explorer*, and Mozilla *Firefox*, powerful online search engines, colorful graphics, real-time audio and video files, and service providers such as *America Online* and *Earthlink* offering flat-rate, unlimited access and high-speed **digital subscriber lines (DSL)** have enticed more and more people to search for information sources online, and schools and universities, government agencies, publishers, businesses, and individuals are connecting in record numbers. Like print-based information, information found on the World Wide Web must be documented, following the same general guidelines and principles as apply to print. Sometimes, however, finding the elements included in traditional citation formats is difficult (see chapter 2), and sometimes those elements, such as page numbers, simply do not exist. The following examples follow traditional formats as closely as possible while acknowledging the unique features of online sources.

3.2.1.1.Web page. To cite an individual Web page, give the author's name, the title of the page—enclosed in quotation marks, capitalizing the first word and all major words—followed by the date of publication and/or last modification, the complete URL, including the protocol (e.g., "http"), and the date of access enclosed in parentheses and followed by a period. If the page is part of a larger Web site, include the site title in italics (see also section 3.2.1.2).

Downes, Stephen. "The New Literacy." 4 Oct. 2002. *Stephen's Web.* http://www.downes.ca/cgi-bin/website/view.cgi?dbs =Article&key=1033756665&format=full (8 Mar. 2006).

3.2.1.2.Web site. A university may host various departmental, faculty, and student pages, not all of which are sponsored by the university (do not confuse sponsorship with Web hosting; see section 3.2.1.14). Likewise, a corporate or organizational Web site may contain various articles or pages. Generally, cite an entire Web site as you would a book or journal, italicizing the title and including whatever other publication information is available. First, list the name of the author or moderator or other person or organization responsible for the site, followed by the site title.

American Chemical Society. *Chemistry.org.* 2006. http://www. chemistry.org/portal/a/c/s/1/home.html (28 Mar. 2006).

When no author or other responsible person or organization is listed, begin with the title of the site.

New York Times. 2006. http://www.nytimes.com (1 Apr. 2006).

Cite individual pages or articles within a Web site beginning with the author of the article or page, if known, the title of the page or article enclosed in quotation marks, and followed by the title of the Web site.

Yang, Rachel. "Household Names in Chemistry." *Chemistry. org.* 6 June 2005. http://www.chemistry.org/portal/a/c/ s/1/feature_tea.html?id=c373e904410482ee8f6a17245d83 0100 (8 Mar. 2006).

More examples of specific types of pages and Web sites are included in this chapter.

3.2.1.3. Web page or site, no title. For individual Web pages with no titles, include the description (e.g., "Home Page") in place of the title, omitting the quotation marks.

Walker, Janice R. Home Page. http://www.GeorgiaSouthern. edu/~jwalker (18 Apr. 2006).

To cite the opening page for an entire Web site with no title, include the description (e.g., "Home page").

Council of Science Editors (CSE). Home Page. 2006. http:// www.cbe.org (25 Mar. 2006).

3.2.1.4. Web page or site, no author. To cite a document or file with no author or organization or other responsible party listed, begin with the title of the page, enclosed in quotation marks, and then list the title of the complete site (if applicable) in italics; the document date or date of last revision or modification (if known); the protocol and address; and the date accessed enclosed in parentheses (see also sections 3.2.1.5. and 3.2.1.7).

> "The Monarchy Today." *The Official Web Site of the British Monarchy*. http://www.royal.gov.uk/output/Page6.asp (7 Apr. 2006).

3.2.1.5. Web page or site, corporate or organizational author. In place of an individual author or authors, a corporation, organization, or agency may claim responsibility for a site (see section 2.3.1.3). Include the name of the group or organization as the author. Continue with the usual publication information.

> American Association of Pastoral Counselors. "Code of Ethics." Rev. 28 Apr. 1994. http://www.aapc.org/ethics.htm (11 May 2006).
> American Chemical Society. *Chemistry.org*. 2006. http://www. chemistry.org/portal/a/c/s/1/home.html (28 Mar. 2006).

3.2.1.6. Web page or site, no author or title. To cite a document or file with no discernible author or title, include the file name followed by the usual publication information.

> nova.gif. http://reductionism.net.seanic.net/brucelgary/Astro-Photos/Nova/nova.gif (10 May 2006).

3.2.1.7. Web page or site, maintained or compiled. Some sites are maintained or compiled rather than authored by an individual or group. The site may contain information from various sources or may index other sites. The name of the site maintainer or compiler will usually be listed after the title of the page or site. However, the placement of the name will depend on whether you are referencing the site itself or the work of the maintainer or compiler.

To reference the page or site, list the title in quotation marks or italics, as applicable, or the description (e.g., "Home Page"), followed by the abbreviation "Comp." (for "Compiled by") or "Maint." (for "Maintained by") and the name of the compiler or maintainer.

> "Electronic Feedback: *CMC Magazine* Visits the Netoric Café." Comp. Mick Doherty. *Computer Mediated Communication Magazine* 2.3 (1995): 41. http://sunsite.unc.edu/cmc/mag/1995/mar/netoric.html (4 Apr. 2006).
>
> "John B. Watson." *The Psi Café: A Psychology Resource Site.* Maint. Nicole A. Cage. 2001. http://www.psy.pdx.edu/PsiCafe/KeyTheorists/Watson.htm (8 May 2006).

To reference the work of the maintainer or compiler, begin with the name of the maintainer or compiler followed by the abbreviation "maint." or "comp." as applicable, and followed by the usual citation information.

> Karjala, Dennis S., maint. "Opposing Copyright Extension: A Forum for Information on Congress's Recent Extension of the Term of Copyright Protection and for Promoting the Public Domain." Mod. 23 Jan. 2006. http://www.law.asu.edu/HomePages/Karjala/OpposingCopyrightExtension (28 Mar. 2006).

3.2.1.8. Article in online journal. List the author's name, last name first; the title of the article, enclosed in quotation marks; the title of the journal, in italics; and the volume number, followed by a period and the issue number (if applicable). Note that no punctuation follows the title of the journal, but the volume and issue numbers are not italicized. Place the year of publication in parentheses after the issue number. When the article can be located from the publication information (e.g., author, title, and publication date) from the main page of the journal, then cite the URL for the main page of the journal, followed by the date of access in parentheses.

> Trupe, Alice L. "Academic Literacy in a Wired World: Redefining Genres for College Writing Courses." *Kairos: Rhetoric, Technology, Pedagogy* 7.2 (2002). http://english.ttu.edu/kairos (7 June 2006).

Some articles may be accessed directly using a unique URL. That is, you may access the article without going to the home page for the journal. You can cite the direct link to the article, but include journal publication information as well. Make sure, however, that the URL will allow access (see section 2.3.5.1).

> Martin, Julia, and David Coleman. "The Archive as an Ecosystem." *Journal of Electronic Publishing* 7.3 (2002). http://www.press.umich.edu/jep/07-03/martin.html (10 Mar. 2006).

Note that, for multiple authors, only the first author's name is inverted; remaining authors' names are listed in the usual order (that is, first name first). See the *MLA Handbook* for more information.

To cite previously published files and documents, list the usual print publication information, including the page number(s) if known, followed by the electronic publication information. Note that it is not necessary to repeat the volume and issue number or date of publication for the electronic version if they are included in the print information.

> Giroux, Henry A. "Slacking Off: Border Youth and Postmodern Education." *JAC: Journal of Composition Theory* 14.2 (1994): 347–66. *JAC Online.* http://jac.gsu.edu (10 Jan. 2006).

3.2.1.9. Article or page in corporate or organizational Web site. If the article or page in a corporate or organizational Web site does not list an individual author, it is considered to be authored by the corporation or organization (see also section 3.2.1.5).

> Microsoft Corporation. "Help Keep Spam Out of Your Inbox." *Microsoft.com.* 9 Mar. 2004. Last updated 25 Feb. 2005. http://www.microsoft.com/athome/security/email/ fightspam.mspx (28 Mar. 2006).

If the page lists an individual author or authors, begin with the author's name, followed by the title of the page or article.

> McCue, Kevin. "Composite Resin Filling Chemistry." *Chemistry.org.* 28 Apr. 2003. American Chemical Society. http://www.chemistry.org/portal/a/c/s/1/feature_ ent.html?id=1eb26468798311d7ec546ed9fe800100 (14 Mar. 2006).

3.2.1.10. Article in online magazine. List the author's name, last name first; the title of the article in quotation marks; and the title of the magazine in italics, immediately followed by the date of publication. For weekly magazines, include the day month and year; for monthly or bimonthly publications, provide the month(s) and year.

> Ragavan, Chitra, and Monika Guttman. "Terror on the Streets." *US News and World Report* 13 Dec. 2004. http://www.usnews.com/usnews/news/articles/041213/ 13gangs.htm (24 Feb. 2006).

For articles that have been previously published in print, give the print publication information, including page numbers if applicable, followed by the electronic publication information.

Glen, Krista. "Stolen ID." *Higher Learning Magazine* July/ August 2004: 8–14. *Teachmag.com*. http://hl.teachmag. com/hl_Archives/ 04/higher_learning_july_august_2004. pdf (5 Feb. 2006).

3.2.1.11. Article in online newspaper or news service. Give the author's name, if known; the title of the article, enclosed in quotation marks; the title of the site or online newspaper (if applicable) in italics; and the date of publication (if available). Next, list the protocol and address, followed by the date accessed in parentheses. Note that, for newspapers, no punctuation separates the title of the newspaper or news site and the date of publication. You may also cite a direct URL for the article, but make sure it will allow access (see also sec. 3.2.1.8.).

Simon, Cecilia Capuzzi. "A Coach for 'Team You.'" *Washing- tonpost.com* 10 June 2003. http://www.washingtonpost. com (Links: News/Archives/) (8 Mar. 2006).

Sometimes no individual author is listed for a news article. In this case, use the name of the news service, group, or agency, if applicable, in place of the author's name.

Associated Press. "A Kidnapping-Murder Suspect Blogged About his Demons." *New York Times* 8 July 2005. http:// www.nytimes.com/2005/07/08/national/08idaho.html (12 July 2006).

When no author, news service, or agency is listed, begin with the article title.

"Study Finds More Autism Among Kids." *St. Petersburg Times* 1 Jan. 2003. http://www.sptimes.com/2003/01/01/Worl- dandnation/Study_finds_more_auti.shtml (14 July 2006).

3.2.1.12. Article from archive. If the **archive** returns a unique URL (that is, if the file can be accessed directly) or if you can access the article from the main page with the publication information (that is, with the author and title of the article or publication date), then list it as you normally would for an online journal article (see section 3.2.1.8).

> Weinraub, Bernard, and Charlie LeDuff. "Schwarzenegger's Next Goal on Dogged, Ambitious Path." *New York Times* 17 Aug. 2003. http://www.nytimes.com/2003/08/17/national/17ARNO.html?ex=1143781200&en=f8c219125e24bdd9&ei=5070 (17 July 2005).
>
> Monastersky, Richard. "Earth's Expanding Waistline." *The Chronicle of Higher Education* 17 Jan. 2003: A14. http://chronicle.com (15 Mar. 2006).

Include document or file numbers if available.

> Ballingrud, David. "The Ultimate Human Race." *St. Petersburg Times* 19 Mar. 2000, South Pinellas ed.: 1A. *ProQuest Archiver.* Doc. ID # 51305939. http://pqasb.pqarchiver.com/sptimes/access/51305939.html?FMT=FT&FMTS=FT&desc=The+ultimate+human+race (15 Mar. 2006).

3.2.1.13. Article in frames. Documents published in frames do not always indicate unique URLs for each page. List the URL for the main page, and show the links followed to access the specific page or file being cited.

> Haynes, Cynthia, and Jan Rune Holmevik. "MOOniversity Lite: The MOO Newsletter (#117)." 18 Dec. 2001. *TTU English MOO.* http://moo.engl.ttu.edu:7000 (Links: Login/News/MOOniversity Lite) (17 Mar. 2006).

If the file can be located within the frame from the publication information, then you may omit the links.

> Kimelman, Reuven. "The Seduction of Eve and Feminist Readings of the Garden of Eden." *Women in Judaism: A Multidisciplinary Journal* 1.2 (1998). http://jps.library. utoronto.ca/index.php/wjudaism (12 Feb. 2006).

If the file is available in a nonframes version or if your browser provides site information for documents contained in frames, you may choose to cite the unique URL for the file being cited rather than that for the main site.

> Kimelman, Reuven. "The Seduction of Eve and Feminist Readings of the Garden of Eden." *Women in Judaism: A Multidisciplinary Journal* 1.2 (1998). http://jps.library. utoronto.ca/index.php/wjudaism/article/view/170/203 (12 Feb. 2006).

3.2.1.14. Sponsored page or site. Sponsorship is not the same as group or corporate authorship (see sec. 2.3.1.8.). List the name of the sponsoring organization after the publication information, capitalizing the first word and all major words. Do not italicize or enclose the name of the sponsoring organization in quotation marks.

> Leithwood, Kenneth, Karen Seashore Louis, Stephen Anderson, and Kyla Wahlstrom. "How Leadership Influences Student Learning." Sep. 2004. The Wallace Foundation. http://www.wallacefoundation.org (Links: Knowledge Center/Education Leadership) (18 July 2006).

3.2.1.15. Conferences. To cite papers presented at conferences that are available online, list the author's name, last name first, and the title of the paper enclosed in quotation marks. Next, give the name of the conference, the location (e.g., city and state or country), and the date, followed by the title of the online site or archive, the URL, and the date of access

> Bruce, Christine Susan. "Information Literacy as a Catalyst for Educational Change: A Background Paper." International Conference of Information Literacy Experts. Prague, Czech Republic. 20–23 Sep. 2003. *National Forum on Information Literacy.* http://www.infolit.org/International_Conference/ papers/bruce-fullpaper.pdf (29 Aug. 2006).

Cite online conferences in a similar manner, including the online location (e.g., *Connections MOO*) and the address of any archives, if available.

> Johnson, Eric. "Writing as Problem Solving in Online Courses." Computers and Writing Online 2001. *Connections MOO.* 26 Mar. 2001. http://web.nwe.ufl.edu/cwonline2001/logs/johnson-0326.html (14 July 2006)

3.2.1.16. Government Web site. List the name of the government and the government agency or agencies; the title of the site (if applicable) in italics, or the description (e.g., "Home Page"); the date of publication or revision (if available); the protocol and address; and the date of access enclosed in parentheses.

> United States. Library of Congress. *American Memory.* http://memory.loc.gov (3 Mar. 2006).
> United States. Dept. of Homeland Security. Home Page. http:// www.whitehouse.gov/infocus/homeland (5 Mar. 2006).

To cite specific files and documents within a government site, include the title of the document in quotation marks, and any search path information or document or file numbers.

United States. Office of Science and Technology. National Science and Technology Council. Committee on Science. Interagency Working Group on Plant Genomes. "National Plant Genome Initiative: Progress Report." 2001. http://www.ostp. gov/NSTC/html/mpgi2001/npgi2001.pdf (3 Nov. 2005).

United States. House of Representatives. Committee on Education and the Workforce. "Teacher Recruitment and Retention Act of 2003." 108th Cong. 1st sess. HR #108–182. Washington: GPO, 2003. http://frwebgate.access.gpo.gov/ cgi-bin/getdoc.cgi?dbname=108_cong_reports&docid=f: hr182.108.pdf (15 Apr. 2006).

3.2.1.17. Online book, electronic. List the author's or editor's name, last name first; the title of the book in italics; the date of publication and/ or revision or last modification, the URL, and the date of access.

Halsall, Paul, ed. *Internet Medieval Sourcebook.* Rev. 1999. Mod. 8 Jan. 2000. http://www.fordham.edu/halsall/sbook. html (24 June 2006).

3.2.1.18. Online book, previously published. Include print publication information followed by electronic publication information, including the URL and the title of the online site that hosts the e-text, if applicable.

Rheingold, Howard. *The Virtual Community.* New York: HarperPerennial, 1993. Rev. 1998. http://www.rheingold. com/vc/book (8 July 2006).

Sedgwick, Catharine Maria. *A New-England Tale; or, Sketches of New-England Character and Manners.* New York: E. Bliss and E. White, 1822. *Electronic Text Center.* University of Virginia Library. 1997. http://etext.lib.virginia.edu/etcbin/ toccer-eafpublic?id=eaf335.xml&tag=public&data=/ texts/eaf&part=0 (19 July 2006).

3.2.1.19. Web page or site, revised or modified. Include the date of revision preceded by the abbreviation "Rev." or the date of last modification preceded by the abbreviation "Mod." following the date of initial publication (if known).

> Golombek, M., and Tim Parker. "PIGWAD: Layers in Motion." 21 Dec. 2000. *Science for a Changing World.* United States Geological Survey. Mod. 21 Apr. 2003. http://webgis. wr.usgs.gov/mer/revised_ellipse.htm (24 Mar. 2006).
> Australia. Dept. of Health and Ageing. "Population Ageing Policy." Last updated 25 Feb. 2005. http://www.ageing. health.gov.au/ofoa/agepolicy/index.htm (20 Feb. 2006).

In some cases, the date of revision or last modification may be the only publication date available.

3.2.1.20. Web page or site, edition or version. Insert edition or version numbers preceded by the abbreviation "Vers." immediately following the title and before any publication, revision, or modification dates. Generally, if the version or edition is the first, the version number is omitted from the citation.

> Lynch, Patrick, and Sarah Horton. *Web Style Guide* 2nd ed. 2002. Last update 12 Jul. 2005. http://www.webstyleguide. com (28 Mar. 2006).
> Tilton, James Eric. "Composing Good HTML." Vers. 2.0.20. Mod. 20 May 2002. http://www.ology.org/tilt/cgh (5 Aug. 2005).

If the version number is part of the title, do not repeat it.

> W3C. "Web Content Accessibility Guidelines 2.0." Ed. Ben Caldwell, Wendy Chisholm, Gregg Vanderheiden, and Jason White. Rev. 24 June 2003. http://www.w3.org/ TR/2003/WD-WCAG20-20030624 (24 Mar. 2006).

3.2.1.21. Links, anchors, or search-path information. To cite an article or a Web site or page as a link from another source, include the information on the article or page, followed by the information on the site or page from which it is linked. Include link names or path following the URL.

> International Human Genome Sequencing Consortium. "Initial Sequencing and Analysis of the Human Genome." *Nature: International Weekly Journal of Science* 409 (2001): 860–921. *Crossref.org.* http://crossref.org (Links: For Researchers/DOI Resolver/). DOI:10.1038/35057062 (25 Aug. 2006).

Some sites offer opportunities to append comments to a text. Cite these files as links, giving the name of the author of the linked file (if known); the title of the link, enclosed in quotation marks; and the publication date (if applicable). Next give the title of the site containing the link (if applicable), enclosed in quotation marks and preceded by "Lkd. in," and continue with the usual publication information, including the path or links followed to access the specific file, enclosed in parentheses, and concluding with the date of access, also enclosed in parentheses.

> Nellen, Ted. "You Are Terrified of Your Own Children." Lkd. in "Declaration of Independence for Cyberspace." By John Perry Barlow. *Rhetnet* 8 Feb. 1996. http://www.missouri. edu/~rhetnet (Links: Snapshots/Declaration of Independence for Cyberspace/You are terrified of your own children) (3 Aug. 2005).

Some WWW pages include links, called anchors, usually denoted by a pound sign ("#") and text after the file name in the URL, which designate a specific location in a text. When citing a specific note reference in a WWW document, include the exact location of the reference within the document.

W3C. "Normative References." *XHTML 1.1—Module-based XHTML*. 31 May 2001. http://www.w3.org/TR/2001/REC-xhtml11-20010531/references.html#a_normrefs (15 Mar. 2006).

To cite a specific section of a text as a link instead, list the URL for the entire document, followed by the linked text enclosed in parentheses.

W3C. "Normative References." *XHTML 1.1—Module-based XHTML*. 31 May 2001. http://www.w3.org/TR/2001/REC-xhtml11-20010531/ (Links: Table of Contents/Normative References) (15 Mar. 2006).

Include information about keywords if applicable following the URL or name of information service.

Healthwise, Inc. "Acupuncture." 2003. Mod. 10 Nov. 2005. *WebMD with AOL Health. America Online* (Keyword: acupuncture) (23 Mar. 2006).

3.2.1.22. Graphics, audio, and video files. It is just as important to cite any graphics, audio, or video files, including podcasts or other multimedia files, which are used or referenced as it is to cite text files. However, it may be even more difficult to locate the necessary information, such as the name of the artist, the date of creation, or the file's URL. The form of your citation will depend on what information about the file you are able to determine and whether your reference is to the file itself or to the page on which the file is published. Also see section 3.1.7 for information on citing graphics included in your own work but not referenced in your text.

If your reference is to the file in the context of the WWW page on which it is published, then provide information about the file as well as about the Web page or site on which it resides. Notice that the titles of works of art are italicized; the titles of other types of graphics, such as maps and photographs, are enclosed in quotation marks.

CBS News. "MLK Jr.'s Legacy." *CBS Evening News.* 16 Jan. 2006. http://www.cbsnews.com (Keyword: Videos/MLK) (24 Mar. 2006).

Leyster, Judith. *The Concert.* c. 1633. "The Permanent Collection: The Sixteenth and Seventeenth Centuries." National Museum of Women in the Arts. http://www.nmwa.org/collection/detail.asp?WorkID=4968 (3 Aug. 2006).

boggsr. "Introduction to Lesson Plans." 16 Mar. 2006. *Evoca. com.* http://www.evoca.com/boggsr (29 Mar. 2006).

Morning Edition. National Public Radio. 11 Apr. 2005. http:/www.npr.org (Links: Archives/Browse the Archives/11 April 2005/Morning Edition/Listen to the Entire Show) (19 Feb. 2006).

ESPN Radio Daily. "Favre Mulls Retirement." 30 Jan. 2006. *ESPN Radio Podcast.* http://sports.espn.go.com/espn/news/story?id=2092153 (31 Jan. 2006).

For files without titles, use the file name instead.

nova.gif. http://reductionism.net.seanic.net/brucelgary/Astro-Photos/Nova/nova.gif (10 May 2006).

3.2.1.23. Document information, source code, and miscellaneous information. Some browsers will give information on WWW documents that may not be published on the page itself. To cite document information screens, list the information for the page, but with the addition of the words "Document Information" after the author's name or, if no author is listed, after the title.

Nelson, Theodor Holm. Document Information. "Transcopyright: Pre-Permission for Virtual Republishing." 1995.

Mod. 14 Oct. 1998. http://www.xanadu.com.au/ted/trans-copyright/transcopy.html (3 Mar. 2006).

To cite the source code for a document or file, cite the document page or file as you would normally, but include the words "Source Code" after the author's name or, if no author is listed, after the title of the page.

Starling, Andrew. Source Code. "JavaScript for Non-Programmers." 13 May 2002. *Web Developer's Virtual Library.* http://www.wdvl.com/Authoring/JavaScript/NonProgrammers (8 Aug. 2006).

Many browsers and client programs used to access the World Wide Web contain information of their own that may be important. For instance, some WWW documents and files refer specifically to the browser software or settings necessary to access them adequately. A site may stipulate, for example, "Best Viewed with Windows Explorer 6" or "JAVA Enhanced" or "Apple QuickTime Movies." For most multimedia miles, the file extension in the Internet address or file name (such as .mov for video files) will be enough; however, include whatever information is necessary to aid the reader in finding the source and to give sufficient credit to your sources. See also section 3.2.4.1 on software programs for more information.

3.2.2. Electronic Databases and Reference Works

Computerized library catalogs may include sources from online information services that are only available by subscription, or your library may have subscriptions to CD-ROM information services. Other databases may be available through subscriber services or on the World Wide Web either for free or for a fee. Likewise, many reference works are available in digital formats. Include in citations as much information as possible on the software or information service used to access the information, including the name of the database and publisher, the software publisher, or the URL, as appropriate, to allow researchers to arrange for access if necessary.

3.2.2.1. Article from library database, full-text. Many libraries offer patrons access to the full text of articles in journals, newspapers, and other publications through searchable databases. These may be accessed through the library's Web portal (as a link from the library's home page, for example) or through the database publisher's Web site, using a password. Cite the article as you would the same article in a print publication, listing the author's name; the title of the work, in quotation marks or italics as appropriate; and any publication information (if applicable). Follow with the title of the database or information service, in italics; the publisher or retrieval service or the **Internet protocol** and address (if applicable); and, in parentheses, the date of access. Include any file or document numbers if available.

> Burman, Sondra, and Paula Allen-Meares. "Neglected Victims of Murder: Children's Witness to Parental Homicide." *Social Work* 39.1(1994): 28–34. *Academic Search Premier.* EbscoHost. AN #9403302574 (25 July 2006).

3.2.2.2. Abstracts or reviews from library database. Many databases offer only abstracts, or summaries, of information contained in articles. Include the word "Abstract" in the citation before the title information.

> Magnus, Amy Lynn. Abstract. "Inquisitive Pattern Recognition." Diss. Air Force Institute of Technology, 2003. *ProQuest Dissertations and Theses.* ProQuest. ISBN 0493980474 (5 July 2006).

For book reviews, begin with the name of the reviewer, if known, and the title of the review, enclosed in quotation marks, if different from the title of the work being reviewed. Next, include the abbreviation "Rev. of" followed by the title of the book in italics, the author's name, and publication information.

> Whittington-Egan, Richard. "Rejoice to Read *Joyce* Anew." Rev. of *James Joyce: The Years of Growth*, by Peter Costello and Kyle Cathie. *Contemporary Review* Aug. 1993: 108. *Academic Search Premier.* EbscoHost. AN #9312030327 (1 May 2006).
>
> Berendsohn, Roy. Rev. of *How to Build a Shed*, by Joseph Truini. *Popular Mechanics* August 2003: 92. *Academic Search Premier.* EbscoHost. AN #10278037 (24 June 2006).
>
> Rev. of *The Heart of a Woman*, by Maya Angelou. *Kirkus Reviews* 1 Oct. 1981. *Book Index with Reviews.* EbscoHost (25 Mar. 2006).

3.2.2.3. Article or abstract from CD-ROM publication. Some books and reference sources are published on CD-ROM or diskettes or may be available only from certain computer terminals. List the author's name, last name first; the title of the article in quotation marks; the title of the publication in italics; any version or edition numbers; series name (if applicable); and publication information (if available). Note that for this type of publication, the date of access is not included (see also chapter 2).

> Pearson Education. "What Is Plagiarism?" *Avoiding Plagiarism.* New York: Longman, 2002.

3.2.2.4. Online encyclopedias, dictionaries, and thesauri. Many reference works are now online, including interactive encyclopedias, thesauri, and style manuals. Some of these are available only through subscriber services, such as **Bulletin Board Services**

(BBS) or library portals, while others are free for anyone to access. It is essential to distinguish among Internet sources, BBS or information services, and other subscriber services. Include information about the service providing the reference source following the publication information. Include any links necessary to access the source, separating links with a forward slash mark ("/") (see also section 3.2.1.21).

> Beasley, Maurine H. "Eleanor Roosevelt." *World Book Online Reference Center.* 2006. *America Online* (Links: Research and Learn/References/Encyclopedia) (24 Mar. 2006).
>
> Brogaard, Berit, and Joe Salerno. "Fitch's Paradox of Knowability." *The Stanford Encyclopedia of Philosophy.* Ed. Edward N. Zalta. Summer 2004. http://plato.stanford.edu/entries/fitch-paradox (23 Mar. 2006).
>
> "Seismology." *Encyclopaedia Britannica.* 2006. *Encyclopaedia Britannica Online.* http://search.eb.com/eb/article-9066634 (30 Mar. 2006).
>
> Nelles, William. "J. P. Donleavy." *Dictionary of Literary Biography.* Vol. 173. American Novelists since World War II. 5th Series. Ed. James R. Giles and Wanda H. Giles. Normal, IL: Northern Illinois University, The Gale Group, 1996. 73–83. *Dictionary of Literary Biography.* Gale Literary Databases. http://www.galenet.com (30 Mar. 2006).

3.2.2.5. Other online reference works. Reference sources may be available online through your library's portal, through an information or subscriber service, or on the World Wide Web. Include as much access information as possible.

> SparkNotes. "SparkNote on Daisy Miller." *SparkNotes.* http://www.sparknotes.com/lit/daisy. *America Online* (Keyword: sparknotes AND daisy miller) (27 July 2006).

"Rosicrucian." *Merriam-Webster Online Dictionary. Merriam-Webster OnLine.* 2005–2006. http://www.m-w.com (13 Apr. 2006).

3.2.3. Synchronous and Asynchronous Communications

Electronic mail (email), electronic discussion lists, newsgroups, and other asynchronous discussion forums such as **blogs** and **wikis** all follow similar formats for citation. Messages are often brief or are personal messages between users, but a number are posted to large discussion groups and may contain valuable information. Traditionally, personal letters are not cited in most bibliographic formats; however, the nature of many public electronic mailing lists constitutes publication, and they should therefore be cited. Even personal messages may sometimes be considered published; however, personal email addresses should be omitted from bibliographic references, and you may wish to request permission from the author to cite the message.

3.2.3.1. Personal email. Cite the author's name (if known) or the author's email or login name (the part of the email address before the "@" sign), followed by the subject line of the posting enclosed in quotation marks and include the description (e.g., "Personal Email"). Note that you may omit the publication date for most personal email if it is the same as the date of access.

Brown, Barry. "Virtual Reality." Personal email (25 Jan. 2006). jwalker. "Citing Electronic Sources." Personal email (12 Aug. 2006).

3.2.3.2. Mailing lists. Include the name and address of the mailing list. Since mailing lists may archive information, include the date of posting even when it is the same as the date of access. For messages retrieved from an archive site, include the title and address of the archive. Also see section 3.2.4.2 for information on citing mailing lists in **courseware** packages such as WebCT or Blackboard; see section 3.2.3.5 for how to cite MOO mailing lists.

Ball, Cheryl E. "Defining New Media." 31 Mar. 2004. *Writing Program Administration.* WPA-L@asu.edu. *Archives of WPA-L@asu.edu.* http://lists.asu.edu/archives/wpa-l.html (20 July 2006).

Hawthorne, Joan. "Re: Survey Research Methods." 8 Aug. 2003. *Writing Center Mailing List.* wcenter@lyris.ttu.edu (8 Aug. 2003).

3.2.3.3. Newsgroups. Give the author's name (if known) or alias; the subject line from the message, enclosed in quotation marks; and the date of the message if different from the date accessed. Then list the title of the newsgroup (if different from the URL) in italics, followed by the protocol (e.g., "news") and address of the newsgroup or archive site and the date accessed.

Allen, Tom. "What Medical Evidence Is Used to Evaluate Social Security Disability Cases?" 21 Aug. 2003. *misc. health.arthritis. Google Groups.* http://groups.google.com (23 Aug. 2006).

Padgett, James. "Architectural Drafting Programs for Auto-CAD and LT." 26 Mar. 2005. news:alt.architecture.alternative (9 May 2006).

3.2.3.4. Blogs and wikis. Cite Blogs or wikis similarly to newsgroups, including the name (or alias) of the author, the title of the posting (if applicable), the title of the site, the date of posting, and the address of the site.

Bartow, Ann. "Parody Is Fair Use!" *Sivacracy.net.* 26 Mar. 2006. http://www.nyu.edu/classes/siva (30 Mar. 2006).

Kiwi. "Re: How Do You Cite a Blog Post in Your Bibliography?" *Kairosnews: A Weblog for Discussing Rhetoric, Technology, and Pedagogy.* 30 Apr. 2003. http://kairosnews. org/node/view/1830#comment (30 July 2006).

"Copyright." *Wikipedia.* Last mod. 29 Mar. 2006. http:// en.wikipedia.org/wiki/Copyright (30 Mar. 2006).

3.2.3.5. Chats. There are many different types of chat rooms, some freely available on the World Wide Web, some available only to subscribers to a bulletin board or information service such as *America Online*, and some available only to registered participants in a course or other online venue (such as WebCT or Blackboard). Many personal conversations, even conversations that take place electronically, do not appear in bibliographic lists. Instead, identify the information in the body of the text as "personal communication" (see section 3.1.8 for more information). When transcripts of conversations are available online, list the name of the speaker; the title of the conversation (if applicable), enclosed in quotation marks; the name of the chat room or description of the conversation; and the date of the conversation. Include information about the archive including the title of the site, in italics; the URL; and the date of access.

Day, Michael. "The Graduate Research Network, Computers and Writing, and Graduate Education." *TechRhet Thursday Night MOO.* 15 Aug. 2002. In "Graduate Education and Computers and Writing: Beyond the Graduate Research Network." By Janice R. Walker, coord. *Kairos* 7.3 (2002). http://english.ttu.edu/kairos/7.3/binder2.html?coverweb/ grn2002/index.html (15 Aug. 2006).

To include personal communications in the list of works cited, list the name of the speaker, the type of communication (e.g., "Personal Communication"), the date of the conversation, the name of the chat room or site, and any other relevant information, such as links or keywords, that may allow future researchers to attempt to locate the speaker and verify the information in the conversation. The date of access may be omitted for conversations that are not archived.

> Beckster. Personal Communication. 3 Mar. 2006. *AOL Instant Messenger.*
> shoe_polish. Personal Communication. 16 May. 2006. *Yahoo! Chat.* http://chat.yahoo.com (Links: Computers & Internet/Electronics).

3.2.3.6. MOOs and MUDs, online games. MOOs and MUDs and other synchronous communication sites or online games may contain information that needs to be cited, including conversations, rooms and objects (including note objects), command sequences, programming code, or even mailing lists. The form of the citation will depend largely on the type of information being cited as well as on what information is available. Include as much information as possible to allow future researchers to access the original source, if possible.

Synchronous communication sites allow multiple users to be connected at the same time and to communicate with one another, usually by typing text messages (although many sites now allow for voice and video communication as well). Whether you are keeping an electronic log or transcript of the session or simply taking notes, you should obtain permission from participants before using these conversations in your work. Synchronous communications may include personal interviews, online conferences, and other real-time discussion. To cite an archived discussion, provide information about the conversation a well as information about the location of the archive (see 3.2.3.5). If the transcript or log of the conversation is not available through an online archive, provide information about the speaker(s) and the location and date of the conversation.

> Kiwi. "Playing the Jester Is Hard Work." *DaMOO.* 4 Dec. 1996. telnet://damoo.csun.edu:7777 (4 Dec. 1996).

Maxwell. Personal Interview. *DaMOO*. telnet://damoo.csun.
edu:7777 (4 Aug. 2006).

Object numbers are an important part of an object's name in
MOOs and MUDs. In many programs it is possible to change
names with alarming frequency, but the object's number will
always remain the same. List the name of the owner of the object
as author if you can determine ownership, followed by the name
of the object, including the object number, enclosed in quotation marks. Include any command sequences in parentheses
after the URL.

Locke (#169). "Usability Lab (#836)." *TTU English MOO.*
http://moo.engl.ttu.edu:7000 (Command: @go #836) (11
Aug. 2006).
"WWW Utilities (#87)." *DaMOO*. http://damoo.csun.edu/
connect.html (Command: help #87) (22 Aug. 2006).

To cite programming code, give the name of the author and
object number (if applicable); the name of the verb or program,
in quotation marks; a description of the type of information (e.g.,
"Source Code"); the name of the site (if applicable), in italics; the
date of creation or last modification (if known); the protocol and
address; the command sequence; and the date accessed, in parentheses. If you are citing specific lines of the program, include the
line number or numbers in the in-text citation.

"Say." Source Code. *MediaMOO*. telnet://mediamoo.engl.
niu.edu:8888 (Command: @list #3:say) (23 Dec. 2005).

Cite MOO and MUD mail messages as you would other electronic mail, beginning with the name or alias of the author; the subject line of the posting; the date of the message; and the name and
number of the list (if applicable) or the description (e.g., "Personal

Email). Then cite the name of the site; the protocol and address, including any commands necessary to access the message; and the date accessed, enclosed in parentheses.

> Jai (#137). "Going Postal Goes PC?" 20 July 1997. *Social (#282). DaMOO.* telnet://damoo.csun.edu:7777 (Command: @read 1 on #282) (9 Aug. 2005).
>
> Max (#143). "Planet Maps." 31 July 2004. Personal Email. *DaMOO.* telnet://lrc.csun.edu:7777 (24 Aug. 2005).

3.2.4. Miscellaneous

Besides more traditional research resources, that is, books, journal articles, etc., many other types of sources are available in electronic formats. Software or video games may provide useful information or examples; handouts or other information may be included in online courseware; and, of course, files of any sort may be available in various formats. Some of these sources may be available on the World Wide Web, some on external storage media such as diskettes or CD-ROM or installed on hard drives. Citations should include whatever information is necessary for a reasonably knowledgeable researcher to locate and access a given source.

3.2.4.1. Software and video games. When citing software programs and video games, include the author of the software program or video game, if known, the title of the game or software (in italics), the version or file number or other identifying information, the publisher of the software program, and the date of publication if known. The date accessed is not necessary when citing software and video game programs.

> ID Software. *Doom 3.* Santa Monica: Activision, 2004.
> *WordPerfect 12.* Ottowa, Ont.: Corel, 2004.

To cite specific information in a software program or game, list the title of the screen or document referenced, enclosed in quotation marks; the title of the software, in italics; the version or other identifying information (if applicable); the publication information; and any commands or path followed to access the information.

> U.S. Army. "212 Ways to Be a Soldier." *America's Army.* Army Game Project. 2002. Washington, D.C.: Department of Defense.

3.2.4.2. WebCT, Blackboard, and other courseware. Information may be published through various courseware packages such as WebCT, Blackboard, and a host of others. Some of this information may be part of the courseware package itself, some may be written by the instructor or by students in a given class. Other works may also be made available to students within the frame of a courseware package, such as scanned copies of print articles or links to external Web sites. Unfortunately, not all of this information may be adequately cited to begin with; nonetheless, citing the course and instructor can allow future researchers to attempt to trace the original sources if necessary.

3.2.4.3. Online course materials. Most citations of course material should include the name of the instructor, the title and date of the course, and the name of the school. If the material is freely available on the World Wide Web, then include the URL and the date of access as well. Cite the home page for a course or online syllabus beginning with the name of the instructor, the name of the course, the description (e.g., "Home Page"), and the date of the course. Include the name of the department offering the course (if known), the school or university (including the city and state if the school is not well known), the URL, and the date of access if applicable.

Collegeboard.com. "Financial Aid Myths: Don't Believe Everything You Hear." 2004. ENGL 1102: Composition II. Fall 2004. Jeff Todd, Instructor. *WebCT.* Georgia Southern University, Statesboro.

Walker, Janice R. WRIT 3030: Writing for the WWW. Home Page. Fall 2003. Dept. of Writing and Linguistics. Georgia Southern University, Statesboro. http://www.Georgia-Southern.edu/~jwalker/courses/fall03/writ3030/ (1 Sep. 2005).

Cite handouts and other documents beginning with the name of the author (if known) and the title of the document. Include the date of publication if known, followed by the title of the course, the date and instructor, and the name of the school or university.

"Designing Print Documents: Brochures, Flyers, and News-letters." PBAD 7120: Written Communication for Public Managers. Fall 2002. Janice R. Walker, Instructor. *WebCT.* Georgia Southern University, Statesboro.

To cite email, discussion boards, or chat room conversations in courseware, include the name of the author or speaker, the subject line, and posting date. Include any other information that may be helpful in accessing the information.

Walker, Janice. "IM-Speak." 24 Aug. 2003. Discussion Board. General Discussion. WRIT3030—Writing the Digital World. Fall 2003. Janice Walker, Instructor. *Blackboard.* Georgia Southern University, Statesboro. http://www.blackboard.com (25 Aug. 2003).

Sanders, Ruth. Personal Interview. *WebCT* Chat. 24 Oct. 2002. PBAD 7120: Written Communication for Public Managers. Fall 2002. Janice R. Walker, Instructor. *WebCT.* Georgia Southern University, Statesboro.

3.2.4.4. Other electronic files. How you access electronic information will usually determine the format in which is cited. For example, an electronic presentation may be accessed on the World Wide Web, from a diskette or CD-ROM, or through a courseware package. Many types of files can be made accessible on the Web, including electronic presentations, portable document format (PDF) files, electronic spreadsheet files, plain text files, or files creating using a word processor. Generally, the file extension (the letters after the "dot" in the file name) provide the information necessary for most browsers to open the file (for more information on file extensions, see appendix B). Include the URL for files available on the Internet or on an **intranet**, or the drive designation and directories, including the file name, for items available through a shared network, along with any links necessary to access the cited file.

List the name of the author (if known), the title of the file, and the date of creation. Include whatever other information will help to locate the original source.

> Association of Internet Researchers (AOIR). "Ethical Decision Making and Internet Research: Recommendations from the AOIR Ethics Working Committee." 27 Nov. 2002. http://www.aoir.org/reports/ethics.pdf (24 Aug. 2006).
>
> Lehman, Carol M., and Debbie D. DuFrene. "Chapter 7: Delivering Bad-News Messages." *Business Communication.* 14th ed. Cincinnati: South-Western College Publishing, 2005. http://www.swlearning.com/bcomm/lehman/lehman_14e/lehman.html (Links: Student Resources/PowerPoint) (23 Apr. 2006).
>
> Nichols, L. R. "Return on Investment: Second Quarter." 2002. p:\public\roi2q.xls (24 Aug. 2006).

Obviously, no book can contain examples for every type of source that may be available electronically, now or in the future. The element approach presented in chapter 2 along with the examples in this chapter should facilitate citation of other types of electronic and electronically accessed information.

4

CITING ELECTRONIC SOURCES IN THE SCIENCES

Like humanities styles, scientific styles usually follow a two-step process: first, a note in the text acknowledges information, words, or ideas from other sources, and second, a bibliographic entry is included in the list of references for all sources cited in the text, providing full publication information. In addition to the author's last name and page number, scientific styles also include the year of publication either in parentheses directly following the mention of the author's name in the text or in the parenthetic note following the author's name. For example,

(Walker & Taylor, 1998, p. 104)

Walker and Taylor (1998) explain that . . . (p. 104).

The page number identifies the exact location within a document where a specific reference can be found, while the author's last name points to the full citation in the list of references. In scientific styles, the date of publication is especially important as the currency of a work is an important part of determining its validity (see also chapter 1). In-text notes also help to support an author's assertions by pointing to information about the credentials of the sources upon which the author has relied, including the name(s) of the author(s), the date of publication, the title of the article or file, the title of the complete work (if applicable), publication information (usually including the place of publication and the publisher's name or the electronic address), and the page number(s) of the article or chapter, if applicable, in the list of references.

Citing print resources is not always straightforward, of course, but the necessary information is usually readily available. For electronic sources, some elements may be missing or must be translated (see chapter 2). When in doubt, it is better to give more rather than less information. For print-based sources, follow the guidelines in the *Publication Manual of the American Psychological Association.* The models provided in this chapter are designed to work *with* APA guidelines for citing print sources, replacing APA's often-unwieldy and incomplete suggestions for citing electronic and electronically accessed sources. For other scientific styles, you can translate the various required elements of a citation, that is, the author's name(s), title and publication information, etc., following these models (see also chapter 2). For examples of styles using footnotes and endnotes, see appendix D.

4.1. DOCUMENTING SOURCES IN THE TEXT

Parenthetical or in-text references to print publications usually include the author's last name, the date of publication, and the page number of the reference. Subsequent references to the same work may include only a page number until another in-text reference intervenes (see figure 4.1).

Documenting Sources 7

The elements of citation for print-based sources must be translated in ways that make sense for electronic publications (**Walker & Taylor, 1998, p. 33**). That is, such features as page numbering may not make sense online (**p. 35**). Other major styles, however, still seem to support the notion that features such as pagination—or at least paragraph numbering—are necessary even for online publication. Thus the American Psychological Association (**2001**) suggests that authors use paragraph numbers or headings to denote specific locations within an electronic text (**p. 120**), even though most software used to access and read electronic sources allows users to search for specific instances of text (**Walker & Taylor, p. 35**).

FIGURE 4.1 Citing references in parenthetical notes in scientific style.

In-text notes in scientific style, even for print-based sources, can be complex. Authors are encouraged to consult the *Publication Manual of the American Psychological Association* for more information.

4.1.1. Citations Without Page Numbers

Most World Wide Web sources are not paginated (see section 2.3.7). Unless the author or publisher has designated page numbers, then, in-text references will include only the author's last name, followed by a comma and the year of publication.

One fact that cannot be denied is that "We live in an age in which rapid change is certain" (Ambrose, 1996).

Subsequent references to works without page numbers may need to repeat the author's name (see also section 4.1.2) but may omit the publication date. If there are multiple references to the same source within a paragraph, reserve the parenthetical material for the end of the paragraph.

For electronic sources with no publication date, use the date of access, in day-month-year format, using the three-letter abbreviation for months of more than four letters.

> The "@go" command allows players in MOOs to move instantly between rooms (Bartorillo, 3 Oct. 1996).

When the author's name is mentioned in the text, include the publication date or date of access in parentheses immediately following the author's name.

> According to Ambrose (1996), the real technological revolution began in the nineteenth century, not the twentieth.

In place of page numbers, you may include file names in parenthetic notes to denote specific "pages" (e.g., specific files) with a larger Web site. For example:

> Michael Day, a writing program administrator at Northern Illinois University, recommends that "beyond incorporating networked technologies for interaction in WAC/CAC programs, we need to adopt, adapt, or develop assessment procedures for the technologies we use" (Palmquist, 2000, day_closing.htm).

The entry in the list of references for this note would point to the beginning page of the journal or article, moderated by Michael Palmquist.

To cite two or more references in the same note, separate each reference with a semicolon. For example:

(Walker & Taylor, 1998; Palmquist, 2000)

For sources with three or more authors, cite all authors' names in the first reference; thereafter, include the first author's name followed by "et al." (do not introduce this with a comma, and note the period at the end).

4.1.2. Citations with Section, Paragraph, or Line Numbers

List section, paragraph, or line numbers, if they are designated in the source, at the conclusion of the parenthetic note, separated by a comma.

> One important reason for the move to electronic writing is that "it is becoming very much cheaper to store information in electronic form and comparatively more expensive to store it as paper" (Goodwin, 1993, sec. 1.1).

If the author's name is cited in the text, list only the section, paragraph, or line number in parentheses at the end of the reference, following the abbreviation "p." for page, ¶ or "para." for paragraph, or "sec." for sections (see appendix C for more abbreviations). Place the year of publication immediately after the author's name.

> According to Goodwin (1993), one reason for the move to electronic writing is that "it is becoming very much cheaper to store information in electronic form" (sec. 1.1).

Some styles suggest counting paragraphs for electronic sources without designated pagination or citing headings or section breaks and then counting the paragraphs that follow; however, this could be cumbersome as well as unnecessary (thus violating the principle of economy). Most electronically published sources are easily searched using the search or find features in word processors, Web browsers, or other software. Check your references to ensure that readers can locate the cited information; provide whatever information is necessary to aid a reasonably knowledgeable reader to the location of the reference in a given source.

4.1.3. Citing Multiple Works by the Same Author

For multiple works by the same author, include the author's last name followed by a comma and the year of publication for each source in order to differentiate the works.

> Technology education has usually approached societal issues from the standpoint of the impact of technology on society (Pannabecker, 1991). However, technology education must help students interpret technological innovations "in the context of technology" (Pannabecker, 1995).

In the list of references, arrange bibliographic entries chronologically, beginning with the earliest year of publication. The author's name is repeated in each entry.

> Pannabecker, J. R. (1991, Fall). Technological impacts and determinism in technology education: Alternate metaphors from social constructivism. *Journal of Technology Education, 3* (1). http://scholar.lib.vt.edu/ejournals/JTE/v3n1/html/pannabecker.html (29 Aug. 2005).
> Pannabecker, J. R. (1995, Fall). For a history of technology education: Contexts, systems, and narratives. *Journal of Technology Education, 7* (1). http://scholar.lib.vt.edu/ejournals/JTE/v7n1/pannabecker.jte-v7n1.html (29 Aug. 2005).

For multiple works by the same author with the same year of publication, designate the publications with lowercase letters directly following the year of publication (i.e., 1990a, 1990b) in both in-text citations and the list of references.

4.1.4. Citations with Corporate or Organizational Authors

When no individual is named as the author or responsible party (e.g., moderator, editor, or other person or persons with responsibility for the information contained in an article or Web site), cite the name of the corporation, organization, or news service, as appropriate, in the body of the text or in the parenthetic note.

The National Council of Teachers of English (2001) features . . .

In a recent report, . . . (Reuters, 2003).

4.1.5. Citations with No Known Author

When no author is listed, use the document or Web page title or a shortened version of it (italicizing titles of larger works, such as book and journal titles or titles of Web sites, if applicable), followed by the document date (the year followed by the month and day, if applicable) or date of access (in day-month-year format) if no document date is given.

("Copyright Resources," 25 Sep. 1996)

(CNN.com, 2003)

Note that APA capitalizes only the first word and any proper nouns in article and book titles in the list of references and does not enclose article titles in quotation marks; however, in the text of a paper, including parenthetic notes, references to article titles are enclosed in quotation marks and all major words are capitalized.

In "Copyright Resources" (25 Sep. 1996), . . .

Journal titles are capitalized as proper nouns, with all major words in the title capitalized, and both book and journal titles are italicized in the text, in parenthetic notes, and in the list of references. For more information, see the APA *Publication Manual.*

4.1.6. Citations with No Author or Title

Avoid awkward citations, especially for articles or pages without individual authors and titles, by including the reference in the text rather than in a parenthetic note.

According to the Microsoft Web site (2006) . . .

The bibliographic entry for this reference would begin with the name of the corporate author (e.g., Microsoft). Use the file name in the parenthetic note when it begins the bibliographic entry, followed by the date of publication, if known.

The comet's tail appears as a streak of light (01K5_030706_gs1.jpg, 2003).

4.1.7. Citations of Multiple Works with the Same Title and No Author

In addition to including the title in the parenthetic note when you have multiple anonymous works with the same title, you may need to include additional information to allow your readers to differentiate between sources. Include the publication date, if available after the title in the note. When no publication date is available, or when the publication dates are the same, include a small letter enclosed in square brackets after the page or article title in both the parenthetic note and the list of references.

Because he was a Catholic, he was not allowed to receive the degree he earned from Oxford and Cambridge ("John Donne" [a]) even though he later betrayed his faith ("John Donne" [b]).

4.1.8. Citation of Graphics, Audio, or Video Files

How to cite graphics, audio, or video files in the body of a text depends in large part on how they are used. To reference a file published online, include the artist's or creator's name, if known and if not included in the body of the text, or the file name (see section 4.1.6) in the parenthetic note, followed by the year of publication or date of access.

The light curve for the comet Encke, for example . . . (Morris, 1993).

The tail of the comet Encke appears . . . (encke.93oct24.gif, 1993).

Files that you have downloaded or copied from other sources to include in your own paper or Web site need to include the source information as well. You may include a "source" line for each image or file as illustrated in figure 4.2.

Figure 1. Photograph of the Supreme Court (Source: http://www.whitehouse.gov/government/images/supremecourt.jpg)

FIGURE 4.2 Cite the source of individual graphics or pictures in scientific style.

Alternatively, you may include a "credits" page or list of figures. For example, a Web page with multiple images from a free online graphics site may include a note giving credit:

All images on this page courtesy of FreeGraphics.Org, http://www.freegraphics.org.

Web pages may also include mouseovers with credit lines, and images may be linked to online sources. But be careful— mouseovers and links will not be sufficient if the page is printed out, mouseovers may not work in different browsers or with different settings, and even links will not work if the original source moves or disappears.

Unfortunately, as easy as it is to download or scan in graphics or other files, citation is not enough to conform to intellectual property laws. Before using these types of files, you need to obtain permission. Government sources are considered owned by the general public, unless otherwise noted, and many sites offer free graphics files. But downloading or scanning in other files without permission can result in legal penalties, even if the source is cited.

It is usually not necessary to include multimedia files in the list of references unless you are referring to them in the text. That is, if graphics or other types of multimedia files are used merely for decorative or illustrative purposes, then the source information in the label or credits is usually sufficient (also see section 4.2.1.22).

4.1.9. Citations of Personal Communications

Personal communications, such as personal email or other correspondence or chat room, telephone, and even face-to-face conversations are not usually included in the list of references, but they do need to be noted in the text. Reference conversations in parenthetic notes, including the date of the conversation or communication.

In a conversation with participants at the Netoric Project's *Tuesday Café*, a weekly meeting of academics in computers and writing at *Connections MOO*, Fanderclai (personal communication, March 23, 2002) notes . . .

The much-heralded anonymity of cyberspace may soon be a thing of the past, if it ever really existed at all. A frequent lament is that "Everyone wants to see my picture online before they'll even chat with me nowadays" (mbrown2137, personal communication, August 24, 2003).

4.1.10. Citations of Legal and Biblical References

Citing legal information can be complex. In general, for legal references in the text, cite those accessed online as you would those accessed in print. Italicize the names of court cases in the text and in the parenthetic note, and include the year of the case

The law stipulates that states may allow abortions to be performed only by licensed physicians (*Roe v. Wade*, 1973).

For more information on citing legal sources following APA style, see the *Publication Manual of the American Psychological Association*. The Libraries at Arizona State University also offer a wonderful online guide to citing government documents at http://www.asu.edu/lib/hayden/govdocs/docscite/docscite.htm.

References to well-known works, such as the U.S. Constitution, classical works of literature, and biblical references do not need to be included in the list of references but do need to be included in parenthetic notes in the text. Identify any specific edition or version used and include standard identification of parts rather than page numbers.

David appointed keepers of the sacred ark from among the tribe of Levites (1 Chron. 16:4, New American Edition).

4.2. PREPARING THE BIBLIOGRAPHIC MATERIAL

For documents intended for print, the list of references should begin on a separate page immediately following the text. Pages are numbered sequentially and double-spaced throughout. Use the hanging indent feature of your word processor to list entries, with the first line of each entry flush with the left-hand margin and subsequent lines indented five spaces or one-half inch. Do *not* use the space bar or tab key to indent lines. Final published manuscripts are usually set single-spaced throughout (see part 2).

For hypertext documents, the list of references may be a separate page or file, or it may be placed at the end of the document or file. Because hypertexts are, in effect, published manuscripts, that is, made publicly available on the World Wide Web, they should be single spaced throughout. Bibliographic entries in the list of references are also single spaced and do not use the hanging indent feature; instead, you may want to use the paragraph break code ("<p>") to double space between entries, or you may want to use a bulleted or unordered list to format them. For more information on preparing documents in print and electronic formats, see part 2.

For both print and electronic documents, titles of complete works should be italicized rather than underlined because, as noted in chapter 2, underlining indicates text that should be italicized when the technology allows. Hypertext links in electronic files may be automatically formatted by your word processor or Web page editor, sometimes with a different font size or color and underlining, which most readers these days will readily recognize as a link. For printed papers, you may choose to remove the formatting or to leave it as is unless your teacher, editor, or publisher requires you to format linked text a certain way (see part 2). For projects to be read electronically (e.g., created with a word processor or text editor and transmitted electronically or published on the Web as a hypertext or PDF file, for instance), URLs in the list of references should be formatted as links, in conformance with both the principle of transparency and the principle of access (see chapter 2). Do not introduce line breaks into URLs; allow your word processor to automatically wrap the lines, even when it introduces some awkward-looking line breaks, unless you are required to do otherwise.

The basic format for citing electronic sources in scientific style is:

> Author's Last Name, Initial(s). (Date of document). Title of document. *Title of complete work* [if applicable]. (Edition or revision [if applicable]). Protocol and address or *Name of database* and Database publisher (Access path or directories or document or file number) (Date of access).

Omit whatever information is not available, but provide as much information as you can. See also chapters 1 and 2 for more on locating bibliographical information.

Although this basic model can help you determine the information necessary to cite most electronic or electronically accessed files, there are so many variations that it is not possible for one model to work for all of them. The rest of this chapter provides models for many of the most commonly used—and some of the most troublesome—types of electronic sources, organized by the type of information source. Also see chapter 2 for more information about the elements included in bibliographic citations. For other types of sources, you may need to refer to chapter 2 as well as to the models in this chapter to help you translate the required elements of citation.

4.2.1. Web Pages or Sites

Finding information is quicker and easier than ever before thanks to computer databases, the Internet, and the World Wide Web.

Moreover, the Internet is quickly gaining acceptance as a site for research and publication. Point-and-click browsers such as Mozilla *Firefox* and Microsoft *Internet Explorer*, powerful online search engines, colorful graphics, audio and video files, and service providers such as *America Online, Earthlink*, and a host of others offering flat-rate, unlimited access and high-speed digital subscriber lines (DSL) have enticed more and more people to search for information sources online, and schools and universities, government agencies, publishers, businesses, and individuals are connecting in record numbers. Like print-based information, information found online must be documented, following the same general guidelines and principles as apply to print. Sometimes, however, locating the elements required for traditional citation formats is difficult (see chapter 2), and sometimes those elements—page numbers, for instance—simply do not exist. The following examples follow traditional formats as closely as possible, while also acknowledging the unique features of online sources.

4.2.1.1. Web page. To cite an individual Web page, give the author's name, the date of publication or last modification—enclosed in parentheses and followed by a period—and the title of the page, capitalizing only the first word, any proper nouns, and the first word after a colon in the title, if applicable. Give the complete URL, including the protocol (e.g., "http"), and the date of access, enclosed in parentheses and followed by a period.

> Cressia, L. L. (1997). Copyright and fair use: Future of fair use. http://www.cas.usf.edu/english/walker/courses/fall97/concl.html (27 Mar. 2006).
> Downes, S. (2002, October 4). The new literacy. *Stephen's Web.* http://www.downes.ca/cgi-bin/website/view.cgi?dbs =Article&key=1033756665&format=full (8 Mar. 2006).

4.2.1.2. Web site. Often, Web pages are part of a larger site. For example, a university may host various departmental, faculty, or student pages, not all of which are sponsored by the university (do not confuse sponsorship with Web hosting; see section 4.2.1.14). Likewise, a corporate or organizational Web site may contain various articles or pages. Generally, cite an entire Web site as you would a book or journal, italicizing the title and including whatever other publication information is available. Begin with the name of the author, moderator, or other responsible person or organization, if available, followed by the date of publication, the title of the site, the URL, and the date of access.

> American Chemical Society. (2006). *Chemistry.org*. http://www. chemistry.org/portal/a/c/s/1/home.html (24 Mar. 2006).

When no author or other responsible person or organization is named, begin with the title of the site followed by the date of publication.

> *New York Times*. (2006). http://www.nytimes.com (1 Apr. 2006).

Cite individual pages or articles within a Web site, beginning with the name of the author of the article or page, if known, the date of publication, the title of the page or article, and the title of the Web site.

> Yang, R. (2005, June 6). Household names in chemistry. *Chemistry.org*. http://www.chemistry.org/portal/a/c/s/1/ feature_tea.html?id=c373e904410482ee8f6a17245d83010 0 (8 Mar. 2006).

More examples of specific types of pages and Web sites are included in this chapter.

4.2.1.3. Web page or site, no title. For individual Web pages with no titles, include the description (e.g., "Home page") in place of the title. Note in the following example the date of publication is omitted because the Web page does not provide this information.

Walker, J. R. Home page. http://www.GeorgiaSouthern.edu/ ~jwalker (18 Apr. 2006).

To cite the opening page for an entire Web site with no title, include the description (e.g., "Home page.").

Council of Science Editors (CSE). (2006). Home page. http:// www.cbe.org (25 Mar. 2006).

4.2.1.4. Web page or site, no author. To cite a document or file with no author or organization or other responsible party listed, begin with the title of the page, followed by the date of publication (if known) enclosed in parentheses (see also sections 4.2.1.5 and 4.2.1.7).

The OWL at Purdue. (2006). Purdue University. http://owl. english.purdue.edu/owl (15 May 2006).

4.2.1.5. Web page or site, corporate or organizational author. In place of an individual author or authors, a corporation, organization, or agency may claim responsibility for a site (see section 2.3.1.3). Include the name of the group or organization as the author, then continue with the usual publication information.

American Association of Pastoral Counselors. (1994, April 28). Code of ethics. http://www.aapc.org/ethics.htm (11 May 2006).
American Chemical Society. (2006). *Chemistry.org.* http://www. chemistry.org/portal/a/c/s/1/home.html (28 Mar. 2006).

4.2.1.6. Web page or site, no author or title. To cite a document or file with no discernible author or title, include the file name, followed by the date of publication (if known) and the usual publication information, including the date of access. Note that file names are not capitalized unless the original is capitalized.

> nova.gif [Graphic]. http://reductionism.net.seanic.net/brucel-gary/AstroPhotos/Nova/nova.gif (10 May 2006).

4.2.1.7. Web page or site, maintained or compiled. Some sites are maintained or compiled rather than authored by an individual or group. The site may contain information from various sources or may index other sites. The name of the site maintainer or compiler will usually be listed after the title of the page or site. However, the placement of the name depends on whether you are referencing the site itself or the work of the maintainer or compiler.

To reference the page or site, list the title or description (e.g., "Home page"), followed by the date of publication. List the name of the moderator or compiler, followed by the abbreviation "Mod." or "Comp." and enclosed in parentheses.

> Electronic feedback: *CMC Magazine* visits the Netoric Café. (1995). (M. Doherty, Comp.). *Computer Mediated Communication Magazine, 2*(3), 41. http://sunsite.unc.edu/cmc/mag/1995/mar/netoric.html (4 Apr. 2006).
> John B. Watson. (2001). *The Psi Café: A psychology resource site.* (N. Cage, Maint.). http://www.psy.pdx.edu/PsiCafe/KeyTheorists/Watson.htm (8 May 2006).

To reference the work of the maintainer or compiler, begin with the name of the maintainer or compiler followed by the abbreviation "Maint." or "Comp.," as applicable, enclosed in parentheses.

Karjala, D.S. (Maint.). (2006, January 23). Opposing copyright extension: A forum for information on Congress's recent extension of the term of copyright protection and for promoting the public domain. http://homepages.law.asu.edu/HomePages/Karjala/OpposingCopyrightExtension (28 July 2006).

4.2.1.8. Article in online journal. List the author's last name and initial(s), the year of publication, and the title of the article, capitalizing only the first word and all proper nouns. Next, list the title of the journal, in italics, followed by a comma and the volume number, also in italics. Give the issue number in parentheses in roman type, followed by a colon and the page numbers, if applicable. Finally, provide the online publication information, including the URL and the date of access. When the article can be located from the publication information (e.g., the author, title, and publication date) from the main page of the online journal, then cite the URL for the main page of the journal.

Trupe, A.L. (2002). Academic literacy in a wired world: Redefining genres for college writing courses. *Kairos: Rhetoric, Technology, Pedagogy,* 7(2). http://english.ttu.edu/kairos (7 June 2006).

Some articles may be accessed directly using a unique URL. That is, you may access the article without going to the home page for the journal. You can cite the direct link to the article but include journal publication information as well. Make sure, however, the URL will allow access (see section 2.3.5.1).

Martin, J., & Coleman, D. (2002). The archive as an ecosystem. *Journal of Electronic Publishing,* 7 (3). http://www.press.umich.edu/jep/07-03/martin.html (10 Mar. 2006).

To cite previously published files and documents, list the usual print publication information, including the page number(s) if known, followed by the electronic publication information. Note that it is not necessary to repeat the volume and issue number or date of publication for the electronic version if the information is included in the print information. No issue number is included for journals that are continuously paginated, that is, each issue of a given volume begins with the page number following the last page of the previous issue.

> Giroux, H. A. (1994). Slacking off: Border youth and postmodern education. *JAC: Journal of Composition Theory, 14*:347–366. *JAC Online.* http://jac.gsu.edu (10 Jan. 2006).

4.2.1.9. Article or page in corporate or organizational Web site. If the article or page in a corporate or organizational Web site does not list an individual author, it is considered to be authored by the corporation or organization (see also sec. 4.2.1.5.).

> Microsoft Corporation. (2004, March 9). Help keep spam out of your inbox (last update 2005, February 25). *Microsoft. com.* http://www.microsoft.com/athome/security/email/ fightspam.mspx (28 Mar. 2006).

If the page lists an individual author or authors, begin with the author's name, followed by the date of publication and the title of the page or article.

> McCue, K. (2003, April 28). Composite resin filling chemistry. *Chemistry.org.* American Chemical Society. http:// www.chemistry.org/portal/a/c/s/1/feature_ent.html?id=1 eb26468798311d7ec546ed9fe800100 (14 Mar. 2006).

4.2.1.10. Article in online magazine. List the author's last name and initial(s) followed by the full date of publication, the title of the article, and the title of the magazine. For weekly magazines, include the day month and year of publication; for monthly or bimonthly publications, provide the month(s) and year.

> Ragavan, C., & Guttman, M. (2004, December 13). Terror on the streets. *US News and World Report.* http://www.usnews.com/usnews/news/articles/041213/13gangs.htm (24 Feb. 2006).

For articles which have been previously published in print, include the print publication information first, including the volume number (if applicable) and page number(s), followed by the electronic publication information.

> Glen, K. (2004, July/August). Stolen ID. *Higher Learning Magazine,* 8–14. *Teachmag.com.* http://hl.teachmag.com/hl_Archives/04/higher_learning_july_august_2004.pdf (5 Feb. 2006).

4.2.1.11. Article in online newspaper or news service. Give the author's name, if known; the date of publication; the title of the article; and the title of the site or online newspaper (if applicable) in italics. Next, list the protocol and address, including any links or search terms, followed by the date accessed in parentheses.

> Simon, C.C. (2003, June 10). A coach for "Team You." *Washingtonpost.com.* http://www.washingtonpost.com (Links: News/Archives) (8 July 2006).

Sometimes no individual author is listed for a news article. In this case, use the name of the news service, group, or agency, if applicable, in place of the author's name.

Associated Press. (2005, July 8). A kidnapping-murder suspect blogged about his demons. *New York Times.* http://www.nytimes.com/2005/07/08/national/08idaho.html (12 July 2006).

When no author, news service, or agency is listed, begin with the article title, followed by the date of publication.

Study finds more autism among kids. (2003, January 1). *St. Petersburg Times.* http://www.sptimes.com/2003/01/01/Worldandnation/Study_finds_more_auti.shtml (14 July 2006).

4.2.1.12. Article from archives. If the archive returns a unique URL (that is, if the file can be accessed directly) or if you can access the article from the main page from the publication information (that is, from the author and title of the article or publication date), then list it as you normally would for an online journal article (see section 4.2.1.8). Note that page numbers for newspaper articles are preceded by the abbreviation "p." or "pp."

McNeil, E. (2002, February 4). Alzheimer mainstream. *The Scientist.* http://www.the-scientist.com (Links: Browse Archive/Previous Year/2002) (15 Mar. 2006).

Monastersky, R. (2003, January 17). Earth's exploding waistline. *The Chronicle of Higher Education*, p. A14. http://chronicle.com (15 Mar. 2006).

Include document or file numbers if available.

Ballingrud, D. (2000, March 19). The ultimate human race. *St. Petersburg Times* [S. Pinellas ed.], p. 1A. ProQuest. (Doc. ID #51305939). http://pqasb.pqarchiver.com/sptimes/access/51305939.html?FMT=FT&FMTS=FT&desc=The+ultimate+human+race (15 Mar. 2006).

4.2.1.13. Article in frames. Documents published in frames do not always indicate unique URLs for each page. To cite a file from the main page, include the links followed to access the specific page or file being cited.

> Haynes, C., & Holmevik, J.R. (2001, December 18). MOOniversity Lite: The MOO newsletter. *TTU English MOO.* http://moo.engl.ttu.edu:7000 (Links: Login/News/MOOniversity Lite) (17 Mar. 2006).

If the file can be located within the frame from the publication information, then you may omit the links.

> Kimelman, R. (1998). The seduction of Eve and feminist readings of the Garden of Eden. *Women in Judaism: A Multidisciplinary Journal, 1*(2). http://jps.library.utoronto. ca/index.php/wjudaism (12 Feb. 2006).

If the file being cited is available in a nonframes version or if your browser allows you to discern site information for documents presented in frames, you may choose to cite the unique URL for the file being cited rather that for the main site.

> Kimelman, R. (1998). The seduction of Eve and feminist readings of the Garden of Eden. *Women in Judaism: A Multidisciplinary Journal, 1*(2). http://jps.library.utoronto.ca/index. php/wjudaism/aarticle/view/170/203 (12 Apr. 2006).

4.2.1.14. Sponsored page or site. Sponsorship is not the same as group or corporate authorship (see section 2.3.1.8). The name of the sponsor is listed after the publication information, with the first word and all major words of the sponsor capitalized. Do not italicize or enclose the name of the sponsoring organization in quotation marks.

Leithwood, K., Louis, K. S., Anderson, S., & Wahlstrom, K. (2004, September). How leadership influences student learning. The Wallace Foundation. http://www.wallacefoundation.org (Links: Knowledge Center/Education Leadership) (18 July 2006).

4.2.1.15. Conferences. To cite papers presented at conferences that are available online, include the title and location of the conference as well as the title and location of the online site where the paper or transcript is available. Italicize the title of the paper or presentation.

Bruce, C. S. (2003, September 20–23). *Information literacy as a catalyst for educational change: A background paper.* Paper presented at the International Conference of Information Literacy Experts, Prague, Czech Republic. *National Forum on Information Literacy.* http://www.infolit.org/International_Conference/papers/bruce-fullpaper.pdf (14 Sep. 2005).

Cite online conferences in a similar manner, including the online location (e.g., Connections MOO) as well as the address of the site or the address of the transcript, if available.

Johnson, E. (2001, March 26). *Writing as problem solving in online courses.* Paper presented at Computers and Writing Online 2001, *ConnectionsMOO.* http://web.nfl.edu/cwonline2001/logs/johnson-0326.html (14 July 2006).

4.2.1.16. Government Web site. List the name of the government and the government agency followed by the date of publication, if applicable, and the title of the Web site if different from the title of the agency.

U.S. Library of Congress. *American memory.* http://memory.loc.gov/ (3 Mar. 2006).

U.S. Department of Homeland Security. Home page. http://
www.whitehouse.gov/infocus/homeland/ (5 Mar. 2006).

To cite specific files and documents within a government site,
include the title of the document.

U.S. Office of Science and Technology National Science and
Technology Council Committee on Science Interagency
Working Group of Plant Genomes. (2001). National plant
genome initiative: Progress report. http://www.ostp.gov/
NSTC/html/mpgi2001/npgi2001.pdf (3 Nov. 2005).

U.S. House of Representatives Committee on Education and
the Workforce. (2003). Teacher recruitment and retention
act of 2003, H.R. 108–182, 108th Cong., 1st Sess. Washington, D.C.: Government Printing Office. http://frwe-
bgate.access.gpo.gov/cgi-bin/getdoc.cgi?dbname=108_
cong_reports&docid=f:hr182.108.pdf (15 Apr. 2006).

4.2.1.17. *Online book, electronic.* List the author's or editor's name
and initial(s) followed by the date of publication, enclosed in parentheses, and the title of the book in italics. Include any revision or
modification information immediately following the book title.

Halsall, P. (Ed.). (1996). *Internet medieval sourcebook* (Rev. 1999).
http://www.fordham.edu/halsall/sbook.html (24 July 2006).

4.2.1.18. *Online book, previously published.* Include print publication information followed by electronic publication information,
including the URL and the title of the online site that hosts the
e-text, if applicable.

Rheingold, H. (1993). *The virtual community*. New York:
HarperPerennial. http://www.rheingold.com/vc/book (8
July 2006).

Sedgwick, C.M. (1822/1977). *A New-England tale; or, Sketches of New-England character and manners.* New York: E. Bliss and E. White. *Electronic Text Center,* University of Virginia Library. http://etext.lib.virginia.edu/etcbin/toc-cer-eafpublic?id=eaf335.xml&tag=public&data/=/texts/eaf&part=0 (19 July 2006).

4.2.1.19. Web page or site, revised or modified. Include the date of revision preceded by the abbreviation "Rev." or the date of last modification preceded by the abbreviation "Mod." immediately following the title of the work, if applicable.

Golombek, M., & Parker, T. (2000, December 21). PIGWAD: Layers in motion (Mod. 2003, April 21). *Science for a Changing World.* U.S. Geological Survey. http://webgis. wr.usgs.gov/mer/revised_ellipse.htm (24 Mar. 2006).

For some Internet sources, original publication information may be missing; include the date of revision or last modification in place of the publication date if necessary.

Australia Department of Health and Ageing. (Rev. 2005, February 25). Population Ageing Policy. http://www.health. gov.au//ofoa/agepolicy/index.htm (22 Feb. 2006).

For books and other works which have been re-released in new editions, you may include the date of re-release after the initial date of publication, separated by a forward slash mark ("/").

Willis, N.P. (1840/1997). *Romance of travel.* New York: S. Colman. *Electronic Text Center,* University of Virginia Library. http://etext.lib.virginia.edu/etcbin/toc-cer-eafpublic?id=eaf416.xml&tag=public&data=/texts/eaf&part=0 (12 Mar. 2006).

4.2.1.20. Web page or site, edition or version. Include version or edition numbers immediately following the title. Generally, if the version or edition is the first, the version number is omitted from the citation.

> Tilton, J. E. (Mod. 2002, May 20). Composing good HTML (Vers. 2.0.20). http://www.ology.org/tilt/cgh (5 Mar. 2006).

If the version number is part of the title, do not repeat it.

> Caldwell, B., Chisholm, G. V., & White, J. (Eds.). (Rev. 2003, June 24). Web content accessibility guidelines 2.0. *W3C.* http://www.w3.org/TR/2003/WD-WCAG20-20030624 (24 Mar. 2006).

4.2.1.21. Links, anchors, or search-path information. To cite an article or a Web site or page as a link from another source, include the information on the article or page, followed by the information on the site or page from which it is linked. Include link names or path following the URL.

> International Human Genome Sequencing Consortium. (2001). Initial sequencing and analysis of the human genome. *Nature: International Weekly Journal of Science,* 409, 860–921. In *Crossref.org.* http://crossref.org (Links: For Researchers/DOI Resolver) (DOI: 10.1038/35057062) (25 Aug. 2006).

Some sites offer opportunities to append comments to a text. Cite these files as links, giving the name of the author of the linked file (if known), the publication date (if known), and the title of the link. Next, give the title of the site containing the link (if applicable), preceded by "Lkd. in," and continue with the usual publication information, including the path or links followed to access the specified file.

Nellen, T. (1996, February 8). You are terrified of your own children. Lkd. in J. P. Barlow, Declaration of independence for cyberspace. *Rhetnet.* http://www.missouri.edu/ ~rhetnet (Links: Snapshots/Declaration of Independence for Cyberspace) (3 Aug. 2006).

Some WWW pages include links, called anchors, usually denoted by a pound sign ("#") and text after the file name in the URL, which designate a specific location in a text. When citing a specific note reference in a WWW document, include the exact location of the reference within the document.

W3C. (2001, May 31). Normative references. *XHTML 1.1— Module-based XHTML.* http://www.w3.org/TR/2001/ REC-xhtml11-20010531/references.html#a_normrefs (15 Mar. 2006).

To cite a specific section of the text as a link instead, list the URL for the entire document followed by the linked text.

W3C. (2001, May 31). Normative references. *XHTML 1.1— Module-based XHTML.* http://www.w3.org/TR/2001/ REC-xhtml11-20010531/ (Links: Table of Contents/Normative References) (15 Mar. 2006).

Include information about keywords, if applicable, following the URL or name of the information service, as applicable.

Healthwise, Inc. (2003). Acupuncture (Mod. 2005, March 4). *WebMD with AOL Health. America Online* (Keyword: acupuncture) (23 Mar. 2006).

4.2.1.22. Graphics, audio, or video files. Citing graphics, audio, or video files used or referenced in a work is just as important as citing texts, but locating the necessary information may be even more difficult. The form of the citation, thus, will depend partly on what information about a file is available as well as on the use you make of it (also see section 4.1.7).

To cite a graphic, audio, or video file in the context of the page on which it is published, provide information about the file as well as about the page or site on which it resides. Notice that titles of works of art, motion pictures, and records or CDs are italicized; titles of other graphics, brief video files, and individual song titles are not. You may include a description of the file type in square brackets immediately following the title, if desired.

CBS News. (2006, January 16). MLK Jr.'s legacy [Video]. *CBS Evening News.* http://www.cbsnews.com (Keyword: Videos/MLK) (24 Mar. 2006).

Leyster, J. (c. 1633). *The Concert.* In National Museum of Women in the Arts, The permanent collection: The sixteenth and seventeenth centuries. http://www.nmwa.org/collection/detail.asp?WorkID=4968 (3 Aug. 2006).

boggsr. (2006, March 16). Introduction to lesson plans [Audio]. *Evoca.com.* http://www.evoca.com/boggsr (29 Mar. 2006).

Morning Edition [Audio]. (2005, April 11). National Public Radio. http://www.npr.org (Links: Archives/Browse the Archives/11 April 2005/Listen to the Entire Show) (19 Feb. 2006).

ESPN Radio Daily. (2006, January 30). Favre mulls retirement [Audio]. *ESPN Radio podcast.* http://sports.espn.go.com/espn/news/story?id=2092153 (31 Jan. 2006).

For files without titles, use the file name instead.

nova.gif [Graphic]. http://reductionism.net.seanic.net/brucel-gary/AstroPhotos/Nova/nova.gif (10 May 2006).

4.2.1.23. Document information, source code, and miscellaneous information. To cite document information screens or source code, list the information for the page with the addition of the words "Document information" or "Source code" as applicable after the page title, or for pages with no title, after the file name or author's name.

> Nelson, T.H. (1995). Transcopyright: Pre-permission for virtual republishing [Document information] (Mod. 1998, October 14). http://www.xanadu.com.au/ted/transcopyright/transcopy.html (3 Mar. 2006).
>
> Starling, A. (2002, May 13). JavaScript for non-programmers [Source code]. *Web developer's virtual library.* http://www.wdvl.com/Authoring/JavaScript/NonProgrammers/ (8 Aug. 2006).

Some browsers used to access files on the World Wide Web contain other information that may need to be included in a citation. For instance, a document or file may require specific settings or software to access. For most files, the file extension in the Internet address (e.g., .mov, .gif, .ram, etc.) provides sufficient information for most browsers to recognize the file type and locate the correct application to open it; however, you may wish to include this information if it will aid your reader in accessing the source. See also section 4.2.4.1 on software programs for more information.

4.2.2. Electronic Databases and Reference Works

Many computerized library catalogs and online information services and reference works allow access to certain sources of information only to paid subscribers or may be available only on CD-ROM. Others are freely available on the World Wide Web. Include in your citation information about the database, software, or information service used to access the information, including the name of the database and publisher, the software publisher, or the URL, as appropriate, to allow researchers to arrange for access if necessary. It is usually not necessary to list the name of the library through which you accessed a given database.

4.2.2.1. Article from library database, full-text. Many libraries offer patrons access to the full text of articles in journals, newspapers, and other publications. Searchable databases may be accessed through a library's Web portal (as a link from the library's home page, for example) or through a database publisher's Web site. Cite the article as you would the same article in a print publication, listing the author's name; the date of publication; the title of the article; the title of the journal or other publication in which it appears; and any other publication information. Follow with the title of the database or information service in italics, the name of the publisher or retrieval service or the Internet protocol and address as applicable, and, in parentheses, the date of access. Include any document or file numbers if available.

> Burman, S., & Allen-Meares, P. (1994). Neglected victims of murder: Children's witness to parental homicide. *Social Work, 39*(1), 28–34. *Academic Search Premier.* EbscoHost. (AN #9403302574). (25 July 2006).

4.2.2.2. Abstracts or reviews from library database. To reference an abstract, include the descriptor, enclosed in square brackets, immediately following the title.

> Magnus, A.L. (2003). Inquisitive pattern recognition [Abstract]. *ProQuest Dissertations and Theses.* ProQuest. (ISBN 0493980474). (5 July 2006).

To cite book reviews, include the words "Review of the book" followed by the book title, either enclosed in square brackets following the title of the review article or, for review articles with no discrete title, in place of the title.

> Berendsohn, R. (2003, August). Review of the book *How to build a shed. Popular Mechanics, 92. Academic Search Premier.* EbscoHost. (AN #10278037). (24 June 2006).
> Review of the book *The heart of a woman.* (1981, September 1). *Kirkus Reviews. Book Index with Reviews.* EbscoHost (25 Mar. 2006).
> Whittington-Egan, R. (1993, August). Rejoice to read *Joyce* anew [Review of the book *Joyce: The years of growth*]. *Contemporary Review, 108. Academic Search Premier.* Ebsco-Host. (AN# 9312030327). (1 May 2006).

4.2.2.3. Article or abstract from CD-ROM publication. Many books and reference sources are now published on CD-ROM or other electronic storage media, or may be available only from certain computer terminals. To cite these resources, include the location and name of the software publisher. Note that, for this type of publication, the date of access is omitted (see also chapter 2).

> Pearson Education. (2002). What is plagiarism? *Avoiding plagiarism.* New York: Longman.

4.2.2.4. Online encyclopedias, dictionaries, and thesauri. Some online reference works, including interactive encyclopedias, thesauri, and style manuals, among others, are available only through subscriber services, such as BBSs, information services (e.g., *America Online*), or library portals, while others are free for anyone to access. Include information on access, if applicable, following publication information, including any links necessary to access the source (see also section 4.2.1.21).

Beasley, M.H. (2006). Eleanor Roosevelt. *World Book Online Reference Center. America Online.* (Links: Research and Learn/References/Encyclopedia) (24 Mar. 2006).

Brogaard, B., & Salerno, J. (2002). Fitch's paradox of knowability. In E. N. Zalta (Ed.), *The Stanford encyclopedia of philosophy.* http://plato.stanford.edu/entries/fitch-paradox/ (23 Mar. 2006).

Seismology. (2006). In *Encyclopaedia Brittanica online.* http://search.eb.com/eb/article?tocID=9066634 (30 May 2006).

Nelles, W. (1996). J. P. Donleavy. In J. R. Giles & W. H. Giles (Eds.), *Dictionary of Literary Biography* (Vol.173, pp. 73–83). Normal, IL: Northern Illinois University, The Gale Group. *Dictionary of Literary Biography.* Gale Literary Databases. (24 July 2006).

4.2.2.5. Other online reference works. Reference sources may be available through a variety of means—through your library's portal, through an information or subscriber service, on CD-ROM, or on the World Wide Web. Include whatever information may be necessary to help your reader locate the exact edition referenced.

SparkNotes. (n.d.). SparkNote on Daisy Miller. In *SparkNotes.* http://www.sparknotes.com/lit/daisy. *America Online* (Keyword: sparknotes AND daisy miller) (27 July 2006).

Rosicrucian. (2006). In *Merriam-Webster dictionary. Merriam-Webster OnLine.* http://www.m-w.com (13 Mar. 2006).

4.2.3. Synchronous and Asynchronous Communications

Electronic mail, electronic discussion lists, newsgroups, and other asynchronous online discussion forums, such a blogs and wikis, all follow similar formats for citation. Messages are often brief, and many are personal messages between users. In scientific style, personal correspondence is not usually cited in the list of references but is noted in the text (see section 4.1.9). Some electronic messages are considered published, however, such as those posted to large discussion groups or available through online archives.

4.2.3.1. Mailing lists. Include the name and address of the mailing list. If the information is available through an archive, cite the address of the archive as well. Include the date of posting as well as the date of access. See also section 4.2.4.2 for information on citing mailing lists in courseware packages such as WebCT or Blackboard; see section 4.2.3.5. for how to cite MOO mailing lists.

> Ball, C.E. (2004, March 31). Defining new media. *Writing program administration mailing list.* WPA-L@asu.edu. *Archives of WPA-L@asu.edu.* http://lists.asu.edu/archives/ wpa-l.htm (20 July 2006).
>
> Hawthorne, J. (2003, August 8). Re: Survey research methods. *Writing center mailing list.* wcenter@lyris.ttu.edu (8 Aug. 2003).

4.2.3.2. Newsgroups. Include the author's name or alias, the subject line, and the date of posting. List the title of the newsgroup, if applicable, in italics, followed by the address. If the newsgroup is available through an online archive, include the title and address of the archive.

> Allen, T. (2003, August 21). What medical evidence is used to evaluate social security disability cases? *misc.health. arthritis. Google Groups.* http://groups.google.com (23 Aug. 2006).
>
> Padgett, J. (2005, March 26). Architectural drafting programs for AutoCAD and LT. news:alt.architecture.alternative (9 Aug. 2006).

4.2.3.3. Blogs and wikis. Blogs and wikis are cited similarly to newsgroups, including the name or alias of the author, the date of posting, the title or subject line of the posting (if available), the title of the site, the URL, and the date of access.

> Bartow, A. (2006, March 26). Parody is fair use! *Sivacracy.net.* http://www.nyu.edu/classes/siva/ (30 Mar. 2006).
>
> Kiwi. (2003, April 30). Re: How do you cite a Blog post in your bibliography? *Kairosnews: A Weblog for discussing rhetoric, technology, and pedagogy.* http://kairosnews.org/ node/view/1830#comment (30 July 2006).
>
> Copyright. (2006, March 29). *Wikipedia.* http://en.wikipedia. org/wiki/Copyright (30 Mar. 2006).

4.2.3.4. Chats. There are many different types of chat rooms, some freely available and some that are only available to subscribers to an online service such as *America Online.* Some chat rooms, such as those in courseware packages, may require that participants be registered in a course or other service. In scientific styles, most personal conversations are noted in the text (see section 4.1.9) and do not appear in the list of references. When transcripts of conversations are available online, however, cite the conversation as you would other types of electronically available sources, including the name or alias of the speaker, the date of the conversation, the title of the conversation (if applicable), and the name of the chat room or description of the conversation. Include information about the location of any transcripts or logs as well.

> Day, M. (2002, August 15). The Graduate Research Network, computers and writing, and graduate education. *TechRhet Thursday night MOO.* In J. R. Walker (Coord.), Graduate education and computers and writing: Beyond the Graduate Research Network. *Kairos, 7*(3). http://english.ttu.edu/

kairos/7.3/binder2.html?coverweb/grn2002/index.html
(13 Aug. 2006).

4.2.3.5. MOOs and MUDs, online games. References to information
in MOOs and MUDs and other synchronous communication
sites or online games needs to be cited, but the form of citation depends upon the type of information (e.g., conversations,
rooms or objects, command sequences, programming code,
etc.). Synchronous communication sites allow for multiple users
to connect and communicate with one another, usually by typing text messages. Whether you are keeping an electronic log or
transcript of the session or simply taking notes, however, you
need to obtain permission from participants before using these
conversations in your work. Personal interviews and other real-
time discussions that are not available through an archive are
usually not included in the list of references in scientific styles,
but are cited in the text (see section 4.1.9). To cite an archived
discussion, provide information about the conversation as well
as information about the location of the archive. If the transcript
or log of the conversation is not available through an online
archive, provide information about the speaker(s) and the location and date of the conversation.

Kiwi. (1996, December 4). Playing the jester is hard work.
DaMOO. telnet://damoo.csun.edu:7777 (4 Dec. 1996).

Object numbers are an important part of an object's name in
MOOs and MUDs: in many programs it is possible to change
the name of an object (including character names) with alarming
frequency, but the object's number will always remain the same.
References should include the object's name as well as number (if
known), along with any necessary commands. You may include
the abbreviation "n.d." for "not dated" for objects whose date of

creation or last modification is not available. Note that the names of MOOs are capitalized as proper nouns and italicized.

> Locke (#169). (n.d.). Usability lab (#836). *TTU English MOO.* http://moo.engl.ttu.edu:7000/ (Command: @go #836) (11 Aug. 2005).

If the owner or creator of the object is unknown, begin with the object's name and number.

> WWW utilities (#87). (n.d.). *DaMOO.* http://damoo.csun. edu:8888/ (Command: help #87). (22 Aug. 2005).

To cite programming source code, list the author (if known), the date of creation or last modification (if known), the name of the verb or program, and the name of the site (if applicable), followed by the protocol and address, command sequence (if applicable), and the date accessed. If you are citing specific lines of a program, include the line number or numbers in the in-text citation.

> Say [Source Code]. (n.d.). *MediaMOO.* telnet://mediamoo.engl. niu.edu:8888 (Command: @list #3:say) (23 Dec. 2005).

Cite MOO and MUD mail messages as you would other electronic mail, including references to personal communications in the text (see section 4.1.9). Messages sent to MOO and MUD mail lists should be included in the list of references in the same manner as email messages sent to listservs or newsgroups, including the name of the author, the date of the message, the subject line, and the name of the mailing list, followed by the name and address of the site and any commands necessary to access the information.

Jai (#137). (1997, July 20). Going postal goes pc? *Social (#282)*. *DaMOO*. telnet://damoo.csun.edu:7777 (Command: @read 1 on #282) (9 Aug. 2005).

4.2.4. Miscellaneous

Besides more traditional research resources, that is, books, journal articles, etc., many other types of sources are available in digital or electronic formats that don't fall into more traditional categories. Software or video games, handouts or other information published online in courseware such as WebCT or Blackboard, and other resources on the World Wide Web or on external storage media such as diskettes or CD-ROM or installed on a hard drive need to be cited if information from them is referenced. References should include sufficient information to allow a reasonably knowledgeable researcher to locate and access a given source.

4.2.4.1. Software and video games. Include the author of the software program or video game, if known; the date of publication; the title of the program (in italics); the version or file number or other identifying information; the place of publication; and the name of the publisher. Note that the date of access is not necessary when citing software and video game programs.

ID Software. (2004). *Doom 3*. Santa Monica: Activision.
WordPerfect 12. (2004). Ottawa, Ont.: Corel.

To cite specific information or screens in a software program or game, list the title of the document or screen referenced, enclosed in quotation marks; the title of the software, in italics; the version or other identifying information (if applicable); the publication information; and any commands or path followed to access the information.

> U.S. Army. (2002). 212 ways to be a soldier. *America's army*. Army Game Project. Washington: Department of Defense.

4.2.4.2. WebCT, Blackboard, and other courseware. Formats for citing information published through courseware packages vary depending on the type of information. Some of this information may be part of the courseware package itself, some may be written by an instructor or student in a given class; other works may be made available to students within the frame of a courseware package (e.g., scanned copies of print articles or links to external Web sites). Unfortunately, not all of this information may be adequately cited to begin with. Nonetheless, citing the course information, including the name of the instructor and the name of the school (if known), may allow a researcher to attempt to trace the original source.

4.2.4.3. Online course materials. To cite course material, include the instructor's name, the date of the course, and the course title, followed by the name and location of the school, if applicable. If the material is freely available on the World Wide Web, include the URL and the date of access.

> Collegeboard.com. (2004, Fall). Financial aid myths: Don't believe everything you hear. In J. Todd (Instructor), ENGL 1102: Composition II. *WebCT.* Georgia Southern University, Statesboro.
> Walker, J. R. (2003, Fall). Home page. WRIT 3030: Writing for the WWW. Department of Writing and Linguistics. Georgia Southern University, Statesboro. http://www. GeorgiaSouthern.edu/~jwalker/courses/fall03/writ3030 (1 Sep. 2005).

Cite handouts and other documents beginning with the author's name (if known), the date of publication (if known) or the course date, and the title of the document. It is not necessary to cite the name of the courseware package for information provided by the instructor.

> Designing print documents: Brochures, flyers, and newsletters. (2002, Fall). In J. R. Walker (Instructor), PBAD 7120: Written Communication for Public Managers. Georgia Southern University, Statesboro.

Email, discussion boards, or chat room conversations in courseware are not included in the list of references in scientific styles; instead, cite them in the text as for other types of personal communications (see section 4.1.9).

4.2.4.4. Other electronic files. The format for citing information depends on how it is accessed; for example, an electronic presentation may be accessed on the World Wide Web, from a diskette or CD-ROM, or through a courseware package. Many types of files can be made accessible online, often in multiple formats, including electronic presentations, portable document format (PDF) files, electronic spreadsheet files, plain text files, word-processed documents, etc. Generally, the file extension (the letters after the "dot" in the file name) provide sufficient information to allow browsers or computer operating systems to recognize and open the file, providing, of course, that the user has the necessary software (for more information on file extensions, see appendix B). Include the URL for files available on the Internet or on an intranet, or the drive designation and directories for items available through a shared network drive, along with any links necessary to access the cited file.

> Association of Internet Researchers (AOIR). (2002, November 27). Ethical decision making and Internet research: Recommendations from the AOIR Ethics Working

Committee. http://www.aoir.org/reports/ethics.pdf (24 Aug. 2006).

Lehman, C. M., & DuFrene, D. D. (2005). Chapter 7: Delivering bad-news messages. *Business communication* (14th Ed.). Cincinnati: South-Western College Publishing. http://www.swlearning.com/bcomm/lehman/lehman_ 14e/lehman.html (Links: Student Resources/PowerPoint) (23 Apr. 2006).
Nichols, L. R. (2002). Return on investment: Second quarter. p:\public\roi2q.xls (24 Aug. 2006).

Obviously no book can contain examples for every type of source that may be available electronically, either now or in the future. However, the element approached presented in chapter 2 of this book, along with the examples in this chapter, should facilitate citation of other types of electronic and electronically accessed information.

Part 2

Preparing Manuscripts for Print and Electronic Publication

5

THE LOGIC OF DOCUMENT STYLE

Style, in the broadest sense of the term, refers to a wide range of issues and standards for producing documents. It relates to decisions regarding syntax, word choice, sentence and paragraph structure, and figures of speech, as well as punctuation, spelling, capitalization, citation, and document format. Issues of word choice and structure are particularly subjective. Consider the two different styles illustrated in the following example: "I spend approximately five hours per day using my networked computer" and "I live online." Neither of these ways of expressing the same basic thought is necessarily better than the other, and the appropriateness of one versus the other depends largely on context. The more technical and less poetic style would be more appropriate for an application of some kind, whereas the more figurative style might make for a better short story.

The next two chapters do not discuss style in terms of syntax, word choice, and figures of speech; guides to grammar and usage are typically the best source of advice on these matters.

These chapters also do not address, for the most part, spelling, punctuation, and capitalization because other, more comprehensive guides, such as *The Chicago Manual of Style*, have already formulated effective standards for issues of that sort. Instead, we focus on establishing standards for formatting academic work that accommodate changing electronic technologies. Articulating coherent standards for formatting *all* documents, academic and nonacademic alike, is impossible.

5.1. FIVE PRINCIPLES OF DOCUMENT STYLE

Like the logic of citation style, the logic of document style is based primarily on the desire to facilitate the process of knowledge building. Standardized document style supports this process in a number of ways: by providing familiar structures and hierarchies for organizing information so that texts are more readable, by streamlining the complex task of producing documents in a way that saves time and clerical costs, and by coordinating formats among authors and disciplines so that texts may be more easily compared and shared. These advantages help authors and readers to orient texts so that they are more readable and easier and cheaper to produce, purchase, and circulate.

Like citation style, effective document style adheres to the principles of access, intellectual property, economy, standardization, and transparency (see the discussion in chapter 2), although these principles are slightly modified when considering document style.

5.1.1. The Principle of Access

For citation, the principle of access requires that a citation style make locating cited sources as effortless as possible. In terms of document style, the principle of access requires that the author format a document in such a way that it is easily cited, archived, and indexed for retrieval purposes. Thus citation style and document style are intimately connected; for example, one of the primary reasons to indicate clearly the title of a document, the name(s) of its author(s), and the location of the file or document within the document itself is so that it can be cited effectively. One significant problem with much of the material stored online today is that standards, such as those in the following chapters, for indicating titles, names of authors, and section or page numbers have yet to take hold, thereby making it difficult not only to cite information but also to access material in the first place. Another factor contributing to the problem of access online is that institutionalized archives with a high degree of reliability have yet to be established on the Internet, although university libraries and digital consortia are making progress. Authors are often unable to ensure that their documents will remain in the same place for a long period of time—an obvious transgression of the principle of access.

5.1.2. The Principle of Intellectual Property

Like the logic of citation style, the logic of document style also reflects the principle of intellectual property. That is, while providing information about a document such as the title and author(s) is essential to conform to the principle of access, this information also accedes to the requirements of intellectual property guidelines. Thus, documents should be formatted to ensure that this information is not only accessible but readily recognizable, whether the work is published in print or electronic formats.

5.1.3. The Principle of Economy

Document style is also based on the principle of economy: documents should be formatted to minimize the amount of time required to read a document as well as the amount of labor required to produce the text in a readable form or to store the file electronically. For example, authors who incorporate large, graphic- or media-intensive electronic files in their work should carefully calculate download times and bandwidth options, which are a major considerations toward the principle of economy. More broadly and immediately, the combination of markup languages like **SGML/HTML/XML** and standardized style sheets means that an author using such standards can format a document once for all time and most platforms, which is economical to a new extreme.

To reflect on the nature of "formatting" in general and how promising new online possibilities might be, consider figure 5.1. At a quick glance we can tell that the name of this document's author is Brown, that we are looking at the second page of the text, that images of women is the subtopic being discussed on this page, and that the work being cited is by a scholar named Prescott. We can also expect that the information required to locate the cited text will be provided in the bibliography of the document. All this important and necessary information is conveyed through format-ting; that is, it is communicated by means of the shape and location of text in a document. "Economy," however, is relative. For people familiar with academic writing, interpreting the formatting codes (spacing, font changes, etc.) has become second nature and, thus, efficient and economical: a lot of information is communicated with relatively little material to process. But, what if a text could be formatted in a highly logical, unambiguous way so that even the uninitiated were likely to apprehend the text as well as the context? Such document design would, again, be hyper-economical.

5.1.4. The Principle of Standardization

Like citation style, then, document style must also follow the prin-ciple of standardization, which requires that users all follow the same code so that they can understand each other. If authors and readers are to use document style to support effective knowledge building, they must employ and understand the standards on

> Brown 2
>
> in presenting women as archetypes.
>
> Images of Women
>
> A similar view sees Hemingway as making "use of feminist rhetoric of rage, economy of stereotype, and metonyic displacement to illuminate perceived gender and ethnic differences within a society that professes to foster equality yet frowns on difference." (Prescott 177). However, placing women in this almost Christ-like position--the saviors of mankind as it were--is Hemingway presenting women at all? Or is he presenting only male fantasies--the kind of stereotyipcal, mythic female figure that women have been condemned by our society to try to live up to?

FIGURE 5.1   Sample manuscript page in MLA format.

which the codified style is based. Spelling and punctuation standards for the English language were strikingly nascent until the nineteenth and twentieth centuries. Standards for preparing documents have made an analogous leap forward at the beginning of the twenty-first century.

5.1.5. The Principle of Transparency

Document style, like citation style, is, in fact, an abbreviated code that conveys information by using spacing and changes in fonts to indicate titles and subheadings; italics, boldface, underlining, and color to indicate emphasis or titles (or links in hypertext documents); and numbers located in margins to indicate page numbers or section numbers. In hypertext documents, the code may also employ image maps, blinking fonts, animated graphics, sound files, video clips, or embedded applications.

5.2. RECONSIDERING THE PRINCIPLES OF DOCUMENT STYLE

Clearly, electronic and online documents present new possibilities for standards in addition to or perhaps instead of those supporting the principles of accessibility, intellectual property, economy, standardization, and transparency of style. Consider the use of hypertextual links as a formatting feature that can work alongside italics, boldface, subheadings, page numbers, and the like. If both a bibliography and a cited work are located on the World Wide Web, for example, then why not make the reference a hypertextual link to the cited work itself instead of merely listing the title in the bibliography? Doing so clearly supports the principles of access (the cited work is almost instantly available) and economy (the reader saves time traveling to and searching through a print library), as well as those of standardization and transparency (after five minutes online, even novices are likely to pick up on the code that indicates a hypertextual link to another online resource: these links are often a different color from body text and are usually underlined).

For these reasons, we must begin to consider how documents should be formatted to be stored electronically or digitally as well as how they should appear on a screen. We must address a set of new issues that probably never occurred to most writers of academic documents; for example, we now need to consider how to format our writing and store it so that it can be easily accessed and read by a variety of people using an ever widening variety of technologies, including desktop computers, laptop computers, PDAs, cell phones, text readers for the visually impaired, and monitors on refrigerators. This extends the principle of access to mean that once an author composes a text and stores it electronically, that text should be readable, more or less, by any word processor or WWW browser on most computer monitors without the difficult, irritating, and often unsuccessful task of "translating" the text or file. According to the principle of access, not only should new standards for document style allow files to be read by most digital devices, but these standards should permit files on the Internet or the Web to appear onscreen more or less as the author intended when the file was created in the first place.

Thus document style has taken on a new dimension: making files compatible with a wide variety of technologies and platforms. But standards for achieving cross-platform compatibility must also accommodate the needs and logic of conventional, print-oriented document-production styles during this period of transition between a print-oriented culture and a more fully electronic one. In the first two chapters we explained online citation style in terms of the generic components that make up most bibliographic citations: author, title, and publication information. Likewise, document style can also be explained in terms of generic components. Academic documents are typically easy to format because they are fairly austere. The styles they employ are intended to emphasize content and substance over flash. The components that constitute the core of academic document style are basic, hierarchical, and utilitarian.

As we noted in the preface of this book, the standardization of style may seem, on the one hand, like a top-down phenomenon in which powerful authorities determine rules that everyone else must follow. But, on the other hand, if rules or standards are to be effective and take hold, they must reflect the values and identity of a community of writers; thus standards are also determined from the ground up. The world of academic and scholarly publishing has now reached some consensus regarding online style. Large national and international organizations such as ANSI, ISO, and the World Wide Web Consortium (WC3) have been trying for some time now to generate logical, user-friendly guides to formatting electronic texts, and they have had some success in this pursuit, beginning with SGML, which is an acronym for Standard Generalized Markup Language.

The widespread popularity of the World Wide Web, however, has pushed us beyond basic SGML. HTML (Hypertext Markup Language), the first standard for the Web, was originally considered a subset of SGML. Because of the widespread popularity of the Web, however, HTML and its successor/descendant XML (Extensible Hypertext Markup Language) continue to expand in directions far beyond the official limits of SGML. The story of the evolution from SGML to HTML, **XHTML**, and XML is lengthy and well documented in many places. In short, SGML, the parent markup language of the digital world, was too strict to meet the varying, evolving, and revolutionary needs of Internet users. Market competition between dueling browser corporations, most notably Netscape (*Navigator*) and Microsoft (*Internet Explorer*), meant that the WC3 lost control over leapfrogging improvisations on the HTML standard. In response, XML has emerged as the standard, because it is more flexible or *extensible*. XML authors can create tags or codes that fit their needs rather than relying on a strict list of choices (as long as they provide a corresponding file or style sheet that defines their choices).

Fortunately, in terms of producing academic documents, SGML, HTML, and XML are so similar that an author need only understand the basics of either of these standards in order to produce documents that follow the principle of access. In other words, the standards we describe in the following chapters enable academic authors to format their documents in a simple, straightforward way that is compatible with the past, present, and future—the point being that you can (and should) format your document only once in such a way that future editors, publishers, and technologies will be able to access and manipulate it easily.

Most academic authors are less familiar with logical markup languages (SGML, HTML, XML) and are more familiar with **WYSI-WYG** (What You See Is What You Get) document formatting as in Microsoft *Word*, Corel *WordPerfect*, Adobe PDF, and open-source word processing like that in *OpenOffice*. For the vast majority of us who have never worked directly with computer code, WYSIWYG seems like the easiest and most intuitive course to follow, which it is, as long as you only plan to print the document yourself and do little with the document after printing. However, authors are increasingly reproducing, revising, and redistributing their work digitally, which calls for new approaches and new standards for document formatting and production. Further, most WYSIWYG products are proprietary, which means that they are owned and created by corporations that often aim to make their competitors' formats obsolete, as opposed to supporting unified standards, formats, and approaches that move us all forward.

Each of the arguments regarding the primacy of WYSIWYG, SGML, HTML, and XML is compelling, and the question as to which should be accepted as standard certainly remains to be resolved. In the meantime, however, academic and scholarly writers, editors, and publishers need advice on which option to pursue if they have a choice. We would argue that, all things considered, XHTML is, at present, the best option because it holds the most potential for making the possibility of cross-platform translatability a reality in academic circles and because the downside to learning a small subset of XHTML for these purposes is relatively small. If XHTML fails to take hold and another language becomes the standard, the investment in learning XHTML should not be a monumental loss for its users because future languages are likely to encompass, not contradict, its principles.

While the option of sticking with a standard word processor may sound appealing to many authors, editors and publishers are more apt to balk at this approach. No matter how effective or "clean" a program for translating between word processors and desktop publishing software may seem, there are always glitches. This means editors and publishers must develop elaborate and resource-consuming procedures for making sure that translations do not introduce errors, and this can be a nightmare. The problem of translating between word processing and desktop publishing software also creates problems for authors. Because most academic texts are now originally stored digitally by the authors and because rekeying an author's writing is an expensive and time-consuming process, many editors and publishers have procedures they have developed in-house for submitting manuscripts digitally. Before the publication of this guide, no standardization of digital academic texts existed, and authors often have had to take on the tedious and frustrating chore of first comprehending in-house guidelines and then trying to conform to them, a task that must be performed repeatedly because each publisher has different guidelines. *The Columbia Guide* can help solve this problem.

The guidelines that follow attempt to move authors, editors, and publishers alike toward consensus on the production of electronic manuscript submission. Chapter 6 discusses the proper preparation of texts in **hard-copy** (paper) and electronic form; chapter 7 presents standards for document production for materials published on computer networks, especially the World Wide Web. Authors, teachers, and editors should decide which standard (word processing or network) best suits their needs and review the information in the appropriate chapter(s). Standards based on word-processing applications are likely to be, at first, the most accommodating to teachers, students, and the typical scholarly author, although these standards are more limited in terms of transferring documents between applications and the Internet, meaning that such documents risk obsolescence.

At present, individual editors, publishers, institutions, and associations all have their own specific guidelines for producing and formatting documents, and these guidelines must be carefully followed by authors wanting to submit a well-received manuscript. These various guidelines are generally reasonable, well thought out, and useful. They help writers produce attractive documents relatively easily, and they encourage all writers to present clean and neat texts with ample margins, clearly labeled titles, logically organized subheadings, and prudently arranged bibliographies. How-

.ever, in a world where liberality of access and cross-pollination of formats is becoming the norm, it would seem timely for journals and presses to consider adopting a single set of standards—such as those described in either chapter 6 or 7—as their in-house guidelines for submission of manuscripts on disk and in hard copy form so that both authors and publishers can begin to take advantage of more uniform processes for submission and publication.

6

CREATING DOCUMENTS FOR PRINT

In this chapter we define standards for using word-processing software to produce hard-copy (i.e., paper) documents for submission either in print form only or in conjunction with digital copy on disk or another medium. These standards are designed primarily to help two groups of people: (1) students and teachers who exchange written assignments and (2) authors, editors, and publishers who exchange documents and files intended for print publication. (Standards for producing documents to be published electronically are presented in chapter 7.)

Before getting into the specifics of these standards, we need to emphasize a cardinal rule regarding working with word processors to produce formal academic and scholarly papers on hard copy: *In all circumstances, keep it simple.*

For academic and scholarly documents that will be submitted to publishers either as hard copy or in digital formats for print publication, this cardinal rule has two important corollaries:

Corollary 1: Do not use any of the word processor's formatting features unless you absolutely must. This means, do not change fonts, do not change margins, and do not justify text unless necessary to meet the demands of the person or organization receiving your work (for example, text on cover and title pages should be centered using the automatic-centering feature of your word processor; block quotations in print-only texts should be indented using the automatic indentation feature, not by changing the margins; and some citation styles demand centered or boldface subheads). As long as the default settings on your word processor are reasonable, use them. By "reasonable" we mean that the default font should be Courier, Roman (or Times Roman, or Times New Roman), or Palatino (or the closest equivalent, if one of these is not available); the margins should generally be set to one inch on all sides (unless otherwise stipulated in the style guidelines you are following); the *entire* document should be double-spaced; and all text, except for inset quotations, page numbers, and inset lists, should be flush with the left-hand margin (i.e., left-justified). If the default settings on your word processor are inappropriate, change them.

Corollary 2: Do not invent new elements of document style. As we said earlier, academic and scholarly document style is essentially simple. Almost all academic authors really need only three special formatting features to produce a text: italics (or underlining if required to meet publisher's guidelines), automatic indent features, and automatic page numbering. In addition, authors who are required to use footnotes instead of endnotes should take advantage of automatic footnoting features; but, be aware that automated footnote or endnote features might lead to problems if the text is to be reformatted or (re)published by someone else. Authors required to provide bibliographies with hanging indents should take advantage of word processing features that help automate such indentation. For documents to be submitted

TABLE 6.1 Checklist: Formatting Documents for Print

- For texts to be submitted in hard-copy form only (such as academic coursework), use italics to designate book titles, emphasis, and foreign words. For texts to be submitted for print publication, use tags to designate formatting unless otherwise required by your publisher's style guidelines (many publishers require the use of underlining to designate text that will appear in italics in final published form).

  Use boldface *only* in the rare circumstance required by certain mathematical formulas.

- Use hard returns only to separate sections, subheads, block quotations, and paragraphs; never use them within paragraphs.

  Use a hard return and a single tab to separate and indent paragraphs.

- Use a double hard return and no tab to isolate each of the following elements when required: title, byline, notes, bibliographic entries.

- Never use tabs or the space bar to indent a block quotation. Do not use hard returns to separate the lines inside a block quotation. Use the word processor's automated indent function to inset text for print-only texts or use tags for texts to be submitted for print publication.

- If you must move text away from the left margin to create columns in a table, use tabs; do not use the space bar or change the margins.

- Do not center or fully justify text unless absolutely required to do so. If you must center some portions of your text (such as on the cover or title page) between the right and left margins, use the word processor's centering function (or tags for work to be submitted to publishers); never center manually using tabs or space bars.

in hard-copy form only (such as course essays), authors who have mastered automatic section numbering, list numbering, bulleting, and endnotes should also take advantage of these functions, although they should be aware that such automatic functions can create problems for the novice user and may sometimes be incompatible with some styles for citation. All authors should take advantage of spell checkers, although spell checkers will not replace careful proofreading.

For texts submitted in electronic format for print publication, a third corollary also applies:

Corollary 3: If you are an author who has been asked to submit your work in electronic form using a standard word processing application, be aware that every special formatting feature you employ in your text other than italics/underlining and page numbering is likely to have to be removed by your publisher and can easily introduce errors into your manuscript.

Do not worry that important elements of style such as block quotations, titles, notes, and subheads will not be formatted effectively under these austere guidelines. Formatting codes, or tags, are used to designate these items. These code- or tag-based styles replace the standard styles for academic documents that rely on typographical systems for formatting texts and foster easier translation from one application (i.e., the author's word-processing program) to another (i.e., the publisher's electronic text-processing program almost certainly in combination with a style-sheet technology) with the least possibility of error. For example, to distinguish a subhead in the interior of a text, conventional guides to style require that it be set off using a typographical formatting procedure, such as underlining or italics, that is also used for other purposes, such as indicating emphasis or foreign words. A code- or tag-based format, by contrast, is intended to generate a document in which the devices used to indicate different elements of style correspond specifically and logically to the elements themselves. For example, in this system, an author would not indicate a subhead with underlining or italics but instead would surround it with a pair of tags not only designating it as a subhead but specifying what type of subhead it is.

At first, acclimating to this new system for formatting may seem tedious and constrictive, but it will be liberating in the long run. Virtually every academic author knows the frustration of trying to format a particular document to meet the idiosyncratic demands of individual teachers, publishers, and editors. Consider, for example, the different approaches recommended by Chicago, APA, and MLA for formatting subheads in conventional typographical markup standards. Chicago and MLA prefer A-level subheads to be set flush left, in all capital letters, while APA requires that A-level subheads be centered, in upper- and lowercase letters. In a tag-based format, authors simply tag an A-level subhead with <h3> at the beginning of the head and </h3> at the end, and readers, publishers, and editors can arrange the subhead on the page or screen as they please. Thus authors who use a tag-based format need only familiarize themselves with one small list of tags for formatting the basic elements of an academic text; editors and publishers can then easily locate the tagged elements and, using global search-and-replace commands (or corresponding style sheets), recode them according to their preferences.

Although keeping the cardinal rule of word processing and its corollaries in mind can solve a great many problems for authors, editors, and publishers, specific ramifications of these rules need to be spelled out. Table 6.1 presents a summary of the general rules to follow when using a word processor to prepare a document. More detailed explanations and rules for the individual components of document style follow.

6.1. THE PARTS OF THE TEXT

Typical print projects include front matter (title page, table of contents, etc.), the body, and back matter (for example, a bibliography, appendix, index, etc.).

6.1.1. Front Matter

Front matter for chapter- and article-length texts can include a cover page, an abstract, and a preface or introduction. Book-length projects sometimes require additional front matter, for example, forewords, acknowledgments, and lists of artwork or tables. Each element of front matter for book-length projects should be stored either separately as an independent file or collectively in a single file. Material for the cover of a book should always be stored as an independent file, never collected with the other front matter. The other elements should be separated with **hard page breaks** (unless each is already located in a separate computer file).

The following elements are discussed in the order in which they would appear in the text.

6.1.1.1. Covers and cover pages. Covers are generally not the responsibility of the author, although authors sometimes provide dust jacket or back-cover copy designed to promote the book. If this material is to be provided, it should be located in a file or on a disk separate from the rest of the manuscript. Since digital images tend to be relatively memory-consuming, digital files containing graphics for a cover provided by the author should be also placed on a separate disk from the rest of the manuscript.

A cover page is a single page that contains at least the complete title of the work and the name(s) and affiliation(s) of the work's author(s), editor(s), and translator(s). Articles, essays, and chapters do not necessarily require cover pages; the title and the authors' names and affiliations can be placed on the first page of the manuscript. Center all text on the cover page in print-only texts; in texts to be submitted for print publication, however, place all text flush left and use tags to designate formatting.

Because academic papers are often submitted anonymously for the purposes of objective grading or review, a cover page may also need to include information for contacting or identifying the author, such as a postal address, email address, or student identification number. In such cases, it is imperative that the title on the cover page correspond with the title and headers in the manuscript itself. Some style guides, such as APA, require that the running header be either included or indicated on the cover page.

If you must supply an abstract, you will need a cover page. But, in all other circumstances, do not use a cover page unless required to do so.

6.1.1.2. Title page. In book-length texts, the title page contains as much of the following information as appropriate: full title of complete work; names of author(s), editor(s), or compiler(s); name(s) of translator(s); edition number; series name; volume number; name(s) of series editor(s); name and location of publisher.

6.1.1.3. Information page. In book-length texts, the information page contains data relevant to the publishing and archiving of the manuscript. It typically includes such information as copyright and edition information—including dates of publication or copyright—name and address of publisher, Library of Congress Cataloging-in-Publication (CIP) data, and International Standard Book Number(s) (ISBN) or International Standard Serial Number(s) (ISSN). Most often, publishers are responsible for producing the information page.

6.1.1.4. *Abstract or summary.* An abstract or summary should be an informative synopsis that captures the focus of a work, usually within the space of about two or three hundred words. Chapters in books do not need abstracts or summaries.

When formatting an abstract, locate it on a separate page or pages placed between the cover or title page and all following material (be sure to use hard page breaks to create these separations; do not use **hard returns** to move to the next page). Use the word "Abstract" as a chapter head to identify the abstract as such. See section 6.2.10.1 for the treatment of chapter and article titles in both print-only texts and those prepared in digital form for print publication. Page numbers for abstracts often use roman rather than arabic numerals and are centered in the footer rather than being placed flush right in the header. If you must use roman numerals and begin numbering the body text on page 1 (after the abstract), it may be easier to save and print out your abstract as a separate computer file.

6.1.1.5. *Table of contents.* The table of contents, or contents page, is a list of the major divisions, sections, or chapters of a book-length manuscript or long report. It should clearly link the names of the major divisions with either the beginning page numbers or section numbers. Use a chapter head (see section 6.2.10.1) to designate the title of the page as appropriate (i.e., "Contents"), and separate the page from other front matter or from the body of the text with a hard page break (for print-only text), or save it as a separate computer file.

Automatic functions for formatting contents pages (such as the automatic justification feature, with or without dot leaders, to place page numbers flush right) may be used for texts to be produced in print-only formats, as long as the author is comfortable with these software features, but most academic papers are so simple that manual formatting is relatively easy. Always double-check numbers on contents pages before submitting final copy.

6.1.1.6. List of illustrations and figures. This is a tabular list of all the titles of all illustrations and figures that appear in the text, along with the corresponding page or section numbers in which or next to which these illustrations appear. This list is typically necessary only when a manuscript contains more than three or so illustrations. Code the title of the list (i.e., "Illustrations" or other appropriate title as indicated by the style you are following) as a chapter head (see section 6.2.10.1), and separate it from other parts of the front matter or from the body of the text with a hard page break or by saving it as a separate computer file.

6.1.1.7. List of tables. This is a tabular list of the titles of all the tables that appear in the text, along with the corresponding beginning page or section numbers in which or next to which the tables appear. This list is typically necessary only when the manuscript contains more than three or so tables and should be formatted similarly to the list of illustrations.

6.1.1.8. Foreword. A foreword is a commentary in a book-length text that is written by someone other than the author; it discusses the project that follows. In general, code the word "Foreword" at the top of the page as a chapter head (see section 6.2.10.1). The foreword should be formatted the same as the rest of the body text, except that the author's name, title, and affiliation may be placed at the end of the foreword. Separate the foreword from other front matter or from the body of the text with a hard page break, or save it as a discrete computer file.

6.1.1.9. Acknowledgments. The acknowledgments are a chronicle of those individuals, institutions, and organizations that assisted in the creation of a manuscript. Acknowledgments are often included in the preface. Code the title of separate acknowledgments (e.g., "Acknowledgments") as a chapter head (see section 6.2.10.1), and separate the acknowledgments from the body of the text with a hard page break or by saving them as a discrete computer file.

6.1.1.10. Preface. A preface is a commentary written by the author(s) that discusses the project that follows. Prefaces typically contain information about the publication of the text, such as the history of the project, important contributors, or editions or translations of the text; such information may also be handled through an author's or editor's note.

When formatting a preface in a book-length text, use the word "Preface" as a chapter head to identify it as such (see section 6.2.10.1); when including a preface in an article-length text, format its title as an A-level subhead (see section 6.2.13). Use similar formatting as for the rest of the body text, and separate the preface from other front matter or from the body of the text with a hard page break or by saving it as a discrete computer file.

6.1.1.11. Introduction. An introduction is commentary written by the author(s) that discusses the project that follows. Unlike a preface, introductions typically orient the reader to the ensuing text's argument or content, usually including substantial information about the organization and theme of the text. However, no hard and fast rule can be said to distinguish the function of a preface from that of an introduction. It is highly unlikely that an article will require both a preface and an introduction, although this is not uncommon in book-length texts.

When formatting an introduction in a book-length text, locate it immediately before the body text. Use the word "Introduction" as a chapter head to identify the introduction as such (see section 6.2.10.1); when including an introduction in an article-length text, format its title as an A-level subhead (see section 6.2.13). Follow the same general formatting as for the preface.

6.1.2. Back Matter

The back matter for article-length texts includes the conclusion, appendixes, notes, and bibliography. Book-length manuscripts may also contain indexes, glossaries, lists of contributors, and other paraphernalia.

6.1.2.1. Conclusion. A conclusion is a commentary written by the author(s) or editor(s) that discusses the preceding text. Conclusions serve various purposes, among them summarizing and synthesizing important points of the material, emphasizing certain points for effect, providing a structural capstone to the text, driving home a particular point, or establishing extensions and generalizations for further consideration based upon the present document.

When formatting a conclusion for print publication, locate it after all other body matter but before all other back matter. Do not isolate the conclusion on a separate page from the material preceding it, unless it begins a separate chapter in a book-length work, in which case it should be headed with the word "Conclusion" coded as a chapter head (see section 6.2.10.1). When including a conclusion in an article-length text, format its title as an A-level subhead (see section 6.2.13). Material that follows the conclusion should be separated from it with a hard page break.

6.1.2.2. Appendixes. An appendix is a body of nonessential information that may be of interest to some readers but would be, if placed in the interior of the manuscript, more distracting than effective. Appendixes vary significantly in terms of their content. Textual appendixes should be formatted as normal body text. Appendixes containing tables and other artwork should follow the guidelines for artwork in section 6.2.18. Generally, each appendix will be identified with a number or letter; its title (e.g., "Appendix 1" or "Appendix A") will be coded as a chapter head (see section

6.2.10.1); and it will usually be separated from other back matter with a hard page break or saved as a discrete computer file.

6.1.2.3. Notes. Notes are itemized ancillary commentary on isolated ideas or assertions in the body text. Notes are numbered—with superscripts or arabic numerals in normal text size—in order to correspond to references—usually numerical superscripts—located at the relevant places in the body text. Notes placed at the bottom of the page are footnotes and should be formatted using the automatic footnoting feature of your word processor, if available; notes placed at the end of a text chapter or article are known as endnotes. Unless specifically required to do otherwise, use endnotes, not footnotes.

Notes should be numbered sequentially throughout the manuscript. These numbers can begin at 1 in every new chapter if the notes are divided by chapter. See section 6.2.17 for how to treat in-text note references.

For endnotes in digitally submitted texts, avoid using automated note functions, double-space between each note, and do not indent any lines in a given paragraph (second and subsequent paragraphs may be indented). (Some styles, however, require notes to be indented five spaces using the tab key; follow such standards if required.) For print-only texts, double-space throughout (do not use an extra hard return between notes), and format note numbers using either regular Arabic numerals in normal text size or the superscript feature in your word processor.

If you are comfortable using a word processor's automatic footnote or endnote function, you should allow it to take care of formatting the notes for you in print-only texts; using a word processor's automatic footnote or endnote function can help ensure that in-text note numbers correspond with the notes themselves. Such automated features make corrections easier for the author but may be difficult for publishers to translate. Thus, in documents intended for publication, use manually formatted notes if there is any doubt about the publisher's translating abilities, even though this introduces the possibility that note numbers will lose their proper sequencing during revision. In digitally edited texts, some publishers place footnotes directly after the paragraphs in which the note references appear in order to avoid this problem. Follow publishers' guidelines scrupulously for manuscripts to be submitted for print publication.

6.1.2.4. Glossary. A glossary is an alphabetical listing of important terms used in the text. Italicize, underline, or tag (as appropriate) the term itself, and double-space the entries. For manuscripts to be submitted to publishers, separate each entry with a double hard return. Use the word "Glossary" coded as a chapter head (see section 6.2.10.1) at the top of the page. Separate the page from other back matter with a hard page break, or save the glossary as a discrete computer file.

6.1.2.5. Bibliography. A bibliography is a vertical list of information regarding works that were referenced in the creation of a manuscript. Forms and structures for organizing bibliographies vary significantly; however, the entries are almost always arranged alphabetically according to the last names of the cited author(s) or editor(s) or the first major word of the title for works where no author or editor is named.

For texts submitted electronically for print publication, double-space the entire bibliography, and do not indent any of the lines in the entry, unless required to do so. (Some styles require that the first line of each entry be indented five spaces or, using the tab key, one-half inch.) Separate each entry with two hard returns to create extra white space.

For work to be produced in hard copy only (such as most academic course papers), the most common format involves the use of hanging indentation, in which the first line of each entry is flush with the left margin while subsequent lines in the entry are indented five spaces or one-half inch. If you must follow such standards, use your word processor's automatic hanging indent function, if available; do not use hard returns and tab keys or change the margins to emulate the hanging indent.

For most styles, the bibliography for a shorter work (such as an article or essay) is placed on a separate page immediately following the body text. Format the title of the bibliography as a chapter head (see section 6.2.10.1), and separate the list from other back matter with a hard page break. The bibliography of a longer work may be saved as a separate computer file. Note that a bibliographic listing of the works directly referenced in a text is typically titled "Works Cited" or "References," while resources that were consulted but not cited while producing the manuscript are sometimes listed in a separate bibliography entitled "Works Consulted."

6.1.2.6. Index. An index is an alphabetical listing of topics, names, or titles discussed in the text. Each entry in the list is accompanied by a section or page number that tells the reader where to look in the text for corresponding information. For print-only texts, you may want to use the automatic indexing feature of your word processor if you are very familiar with it; however, for manuscripts to be submitted for print publication, it is generally better to format the index manually to avoid problems of translation. Indexes should usually be double-spaced throughout. Use the word "Index" coded as a chapter head at the top of the page (see section 6.2.10.1), and separate the index from other back matter by a hard page break. The index of a larger work may be saved as a discrete computer file. Do not format the index in columns or introduce other special features unless required to do so.

6.1.2.7. List of Contributors. The list of contributors presents brief biographical information about the authors who contributed to a text. Italicize, underline, or tag authors' names (as appropriate);

double-space the biographies; and separate each entry with two hard returns. The list of contributors is generally only required for manuscripts being submitted for publication and should be saved as a separate computer file.

6.2. PRODUCING HARD-COPY DOCUMENTS ON A WORD PROCESSOR

Documents to be submitted in hard-copy do not require the same stringent formatting as do documents submitted electronically. That is, as long as the appearance of the document adheres to requirements, *how* the formatting is achieved matters little. What does matter, however, is the quality of the print.

6.2.1. Paper

Use only high-quality, clean, white, standard-sized paper (eight and a half inches by eleven inches for North American standards; A4 for most others). Do not use erasable bond. Make sure you choose the appropriate paper for your printer type (i.e., laser or inkjet).

6.2.2. Printing

Use a good-quality printer. Laser print is the standard, but inkjet, daisy-wheel, and ribbon (dot matrix) are acceptable as long as the print is legible (for dot matrix, this usually means using the letter- or near-letter-quality setting on the printer). Be aware, however, that high-quality laser print on clean paper allows pages to be electronically scanned more easily, if this is a requirement. Toner cartridges or ribbons must be refreshed if the print is faded, and you should clean the print heads following manufacturers' instructions. Print only on one side of the paper, and do not make any marks on the paper unless specifically required to do so.

6.2.3. Binding

Do not use store-bought covers to bind the pages of a paper unless specifically required to do so; instead, use a paper clip or a single staple in the upper left-hand corner. Plain envelopes (eight and a half inches by eleven inches or A4, as appropriate) or folders can be used to protect a paper that is not handed directly to the recipient, but do not attach the paper to this packaging in any way. Follow guidelines for bylines and page numbers so that your manuscript can be kept in order.

6.2.4. Margins

Use one-inch margins on all four edges of the paper, unless specifically directed to do otherwise. (Some style guidelines or publishers' guidelines may require one-and-one-half-inch left-hand margins; oblige this request if necessary.) Header margins and footer margins, if used, should be set to one-half inch (the usual default setting in most word processors).

6.2.5. Spacing

Double-space the entire text, except when specifically required to do otherwise. Do not use extra hard returns to separate paragraphs, note entries, titles, or other textual elements unless specifically required to do so. For most styles, use two spaces after a period or a colon. (Some publishers may request that you use only one space after a period or colon; follow the specific guidelines for the style you are required to use.)

6.2.6. Fonts

Use a standard font such as Courier, Roman (or Times Roman or Times New Roman), or Palatino (see figure 6.1). Twelve-point fonts are strongly preferred, but ten point is also acceptable. Serif fonts (fonts with "tails," such as Courier and Roman) are generally easier to read than sans serif fonts (such as Arial or Helvetica) and are therefore generally preferred for print. Maintain the same font and font size throughout the text, except for footnote or endnote references, which are usually formatted in superscript, if possible. If you use the word processor's automatic note feature, you need not worry about changing fonts for note numbers. If you are required to format manually, eight-, nine-, or ten-point fonts, depending on the font size in the text, may be used to superscript footnote or endnote numbers. Some mathematical formulas may require super- or subscripting as well; font sizes may also be altered under those circumstances. Otherwise, do not change font size throughout the document.

6.2.7. Formatting Techniques

For most academic projects, formatting is very limited. When necessary to conform to a publisher's or editor's guidelines or a specific style (APA or MLA, for example), use the automatic formatting features in your word processor or use XHTML tags to indicate discrete textual elements.

This is arial font

This is courier font

This is palatino

This is times new roman

FIGURE 6.1 Common fonts.

6.2.7.1. Boldface. Boldface is a formatting technique in which characters appear darker and thicker than normal text. Although it is widely used and misused by many authors and publishers for various reasons, it should be employed only in the rare circumstance of certain mathematical formulae that require it. Do not use it for emphasis or to format subheads, unless the specific style guide you must use requires it (some style guides require certain subheads to be boldfaced).

6.2.7.2. Underlining or italics. Underlining and italics are formatting techniques used for emphasis or to set off special terminology in texts. Use one or the other, never both. Underlining is generally preferable to italics for documents to be submitted for print publication for the following reasons: (1) it is easier for readers and editors to identify in hard copy and onscreen, despite the improving qualities of printers and monitors; (2) authors often do not realize they have failed to italicize either the first or last letter of a word; (3) it is much easier for most publishers to translate from underlining to italics than to do the reverse (in publishing, in fact, underlining usually indicates text that should be italicized in final print copy). However, for documents to be produced as final copy (such as academic coursework) and for texts that will appear in electronic form, always use italics rather than underlining. Underlining has become a standard for denoting hypertext links and can therefore cause confusion.

Terminology. When an author refers to a particular word, phrase, or letter itself, such as in the statement "my definition of *honest* is," formatting is used to indicate such usage. The preferred formatting for referenced terminology of this kind is either to underline or italicize the term as appropriate (following the guidelines in this section), although the use of quotation marks for the same effect (as in "honest") is widely practiced. Mathematical formulae, instructions, and computer code also should be treated as referenced terminology and therefore require special formatting, as should words and letters referred to as words and letters (as in "He misspelled the word by not including the silent *g*") and foreign words other than those found in a standard English dictionary (as in "She used the German word *Ewigweibliche*"). Some publishers may ask that terminology in digital documents be enclosed within the <text> . . . </text> tag pair, although the <dfn> . . . </dfn> tag pair is preferable because it complies with the XHTML standard. (See the discussion under corollary 3 in this chapter for more information on using tags for formatting discrete elements of a text.)

Emphasis. Underlining or italicizing (as appropriate) are the preferred methods in academic and scholarly writing for indicating textual emphasis, although boldface is widely misused for the same purpose. Some publishers may ask that emphasized text in electronic documents be enclosed within the <em> . . . </em> tag pair. XHTML also allows for strong emphasis through the <strong> . . . </strong> tag pair, but such use is typically overzealous in academic writing. (See the discussion under corollary 3 in this chapter for more information on using tags for formatting discrete elements of a text.)

Title citations. A title citation is a reference to the actual name of a source text. Citations of titles of works of more substantial length, such as books, are either italicized or underlined as appropriate; in works submitted for print publication, titles may be enclosed within the <cite> . . . </cite> tag pair. These tags eliminate the need to underline or italicize longer titles. Titles of shorter works, such as chapters, articles, essays, or poems, are typically enclosed in quotation marks (" ") in all formats.

6.2.8. Special Characters

Special characters are typographic symbols that do not appear on standard keyboards but are sometimes necessary when producing academic texts. The most commonly required special characters are accented characters such as ü, é, ç, ñ; mathematical symbols such as ±, ≥, Σ, and ∞; and typographical symbols such as £, ¶, §, and —. Most word processors can produce a variety of these symbols; consult the topics "special characters" or "character map" in a software manual or through the online help function of your word processor to locate information on how to handle special characters.

There are, however, standards for special characters. The most widely used standard is currently the **ISO Latin-1** character set, which assigns a particular code to 256 common characters. Some may be more familiar with the **ASCII** character set, which is actually a subset of ISO Latin-1: it comprises the first 128 characters of the ISO set. For example, the code for the ~ symbol in both ISO and ASCII is 126. The ISO Latin-1 set is printed in appendix F.

Special characters may need to be inserted by hand on printed copies. On disks or attachments to be submitted for publication, you may need to designate special characters with an asterisk or other symbol if your word processor cannot handle them. Consult your publisher if in doubt.

6.2.9. Bylines

A byline indicates the author(s) of the work and other relevant information such as affiliation or geographic location. For article-or chapter-length texts, it should be placed flush left at the top, left-hand corner of the first page, above the title of the work but below the page number and header. Bylines placed on cover pages typically follow the title. List each author's first name followed by the middle initial and surname. On a separate line or lines include other relevant information, such as date, course number, and institutional affiliation. Double-space the text in the byline, and use the same font that appears in the body of the manuscript. Do not include a byline when submitting work for anonymous grading or review.

6.2.10. Titles

A title is the name given to a work by an author. Academic works tend to feature titles that reflect the focus of the manuscript. Titles also indicate division and subordination of ideas. For example, book titles describe the general purpose of a large manuscript, and chapter titles describe ideas contained in smaller units that, in turn, form the work as a whole.

6.2.10.1. Titles for article- or chapter-length projects. Place the title below the byline on the first page of the article or essay, separating it from the byline and the body of the work by one double-space in humanities styles. In scientific styles requiring a cover page, place the title at the top of the cover page, followed by the byline. In hard-copy-only texts, titles for shorter works require no formatting; however, in texts submitted digitally for print publication, such titles should be enclosed within the <h2> . . . </h2> tag pair and separated from following text by an extra line space (i.e., a double hard return). Set titles in upper- and lowercase letters—never use all capital letters—and do not boldface, underline, or italicize them. Center titles on the line for print-only formats, using the automatic centering feature of your word processor; do not change margins or use the space bar or the tab key to center titles (see figure 6.2).

6.2.10.2. Titles for book-length projects. In the case of book-length projects (approximately twenty-five thousand or more words), the title of the work should be placed at the top of the title page, beneath the top margin. In print-only texts, these titles should be either italicized or underlined, as appropriate (see section 6.2.7.2); do not use boldface or all capital letters. In texts for print publication, instead of underlining or boldfacing the title, enclose it within the <h1> . . . </h1> tag pair.

Janice R. Walker
Professor Taylor
English 6700
8 January, 2007
Formatting Paper Titles: Works Composed for Print
In texts that will appear only as hard copy, we recommend that paper titles
be centered using upper- and lowercase letters. The title should be separated from other
text by a single hard-return.

Paper or Chapter Title

Many brief works use only a main title. However, sometimes sub-headings are used to
aid the reader.

Format of A-level Subheads
A-level subheads should be separated from the preceding text by an extra hard return.
Use upper- and lowercase letters.

A-level subheads

For texts that require additional levels of subheads, we recommend
the following formats.

Format of B-Level Subheads
Use upper- and lowercase letters, italicized or underlined (as
appropriate). Separate from the preceding text by an extra hard return.

B-level subheads

Additional subheads can also be used if necessary.

Formatting of additional subheads. For C-level subheads, capitalize the first
words and any proper nouns only; italicize or underline (as appropriate); end
the subhead with a period and continue the body text on the same line.

C-level subheads

Separate D-level subheads from the preceding text with only a single hard return.
Formatting of D-level subheads. Indent five spaces or one-half inch
from the left-hand margin. Capitalize the first words and any proper nouns only;
italicize or underline (as appropriate); end the subhead with a period and continue
the body text on the same line.

D-level subheads

FIGURE 6.2 Subhead formats for printed texts.

6.2.11. Section or Page Numbers

Section numbers and page numbers provide a constant and sequential system for referencing specific locations in a text. Use your word processor's automatic page numbering function to place the page numbers in the top, right-hand corner of the manuscript (in most cases, in the header, following the author's last name or the running head). Unless you are very comfortable using a word processor's automatic paragraph numbering functions, however, manually insert section numbers in the appropriate places, leaving an extra line space before the number. Do not include any other text on the same line with a section number. Number every page of your text, including the first, unless required otherwise.

6.2.12. Headers and Footers

Headers and footers are elements that appear on every page of a manuscript in either the top or bottom margin. They typically contain page numbers and the author's last name or a shortened version of the document title (called a "running head").

Headers and footers should be inserted using the automated formatting function available on your word processor. Headers are one of the few elements that should be justified flush right (against the right-hand margin); footers should usually be centered. Headers and footers should be formatted to appear approximately at the midpoint of either the top or bottom margin (about a half inch from the top or bottom of the page). Headers and footers should contain only the last name of the author (the name of the first author in the case of a collaborative text) and a page number, unless the manuscript is supposed to be anonymous or you are required to do otherwise by the style guide you are following. In the case of anonymous submissions, headers and footers should contain a running head. Note that book-length titles in headers and footers must still be italicized or underlined as appropriate (see section 6.2.7.2). The text in a header or footer should be followed by a single space and then the page number. No dashes or abbreviations such as *pg.* are required to separate the text in a header or footer from page numbers.

6.2.13. Subheads

Subheads are titles that give structure to the text by differentiating among its various segments. Subheads are subordinate to the title of the work itself or the title of the chapter in which they appear. Subheads may appear within segments already set off by subheads, much as subtopics may fall within other subtopics in an outline. Like subtopics in an outline, the level of subordination of subheads is indicated by formatting. But whereas in outlines indentation communicates which topics are subtopics of which, each style manual formats text subheads differently. You should follow the guidelines of the particular manual you are honoring. What is most important is that you format subheads consistently: all A-level subheads should be formatted the same, all B-level subheads the same, and so on.

In texts that will appear only as hard copy, we recommend that subheads be formatted as follows (also see figure 6.2):

A-level subhead: Upper- and lowercase letters, set flush with left-hand margin, and separated from preceding text by a double hard return and from following text by a single hard return.

B-level subhead: Italicized upper- and lowercase letters, set flush with the left-hand margin, separated from preceding text by a double hard return and from following text by a single hard return.

C-level subhead: Italicized, set flush with the left-hand margin, ending with a period, and separated from the preceding text with a double hard return. Subsequent text should be run in. Uppercase only the first letter and any proper nouns.

D-level subhead: Indent five spaces or one-half inch from the left-hand margin, uppercasing only the first letter and any proper nouns. Italicize or underline as appropriate, end with a period, and run in subsequent text. Precede paragraphs beginning with D-level subheads with a single hard return, as you would any new paragraph.

In texts prepared for submission digitally, set all subheads on lines of their own, flush with the left-hand margin. Do not precede or follow them with extra line spaces. Always use upper- and lowercase letters, not all capitals. Do not use boldface, italics, underlining, or centering to format subheads. Instead, they should be formatted using the following tag pairs:

<h3>[A-level subhead]</h3>
<h4>[B-level subhead]</h4>
<h5>[C-level subhead]</h5>
<h6>[D-level subhead]</h6>

Note that the <h1> . . . </h1> tag pair is reserved for book titles and the <h2> . . . </h2> tag pair is for chapter or article titles.

6.2.14. Paragraphs

A paragraph is a group of consecutive sentences, each of which relates to a single idea; sentences within each paragraph are grouped together and set apart from other paragraphs in order to provide thematic and textual structure.

The first paragraph of a text or subsection (i.e., paragraphs immediately following subheads or space breaks) requires no indentation. Otherwise, when formatting paragraphs for a document that will be printed, indent the first line of each new paragraph with a tab and conclude each paragraph with a single hard return. Do not use the space bar to indent new paragraphs. And do not rely on a **soft return** (automatic return) to conclude a paragraph.

6.2.15. Lists

6.2.15.1. Ordered lists. An ordered list is a vertical list of textual items that have a logical sequence, with this sequence indicated not only by ordering the items appropriately but also by preceding each item with a sequential number or letter.

Ordered lists should be arranged vertically, with each item beginning on a new line. Ordered lists should also be arranged hierarchically or chronologically. Depending on the context, each item in the list should be preceded by either an ascending or descending number or letter, although numbers are generally preferred to letters, and ascending order is generally preferred to descending.

Ordered lists in print-only texts should be indented using a double tab (about ten spaces) to set them off from normal body text. If you are very comfortable with a word processor's automatic function for creating ordered lists, you should use it. Otherwise, use the word processor's indent function to change the margins for the text in a numbered list. Do not place an extra line space before the first item or after the last item on the list. Place a period after each number, skip one space, and then begin the text. See figure 6.3 for an example of an ordered list in a print-only text.

In texts submitted in digital form for print publication, ordered lists should be set off from normal body text by the inclusion of an <ol> tag in front of the entire list and an </ol> tag at the end. Do not indent the list, and do not precede or follow it with an extra line space. Each item in the list should be enclosed with the <li> . . . </li> tag pair and flush with the left-hand margin. Do not use your word processor's automated function for numbering lists, unless you are certain that your publisher will accept such formatting. See figure 6.4 for an example of an ordered list in an digital/print text.

6.2.15.2. Unordered lists.

An unordered list is a vertical list of textual items that have no significant logical sequence. Unordered lists are typically bulleted. Unordered lists should be arranged vertically, with each item beginning on a new line. Unordered lists are not hierarchical or chronological; each item on the list is more or less as important as any other item on the list. Consequently, unordered lists are bulleted, whereas ordered lists have numbers or letters that reflect

Walker 5

Ordered lists should be arranged vertically, with each item beginning on a new line. Depending on the context, each item on the list should be preceded by either an ascending or descending number.

1. Woke up
2. Took a shower
3. Went to work
4. Ate lunch
5. Went home

Ordered lists in print-only texts should be indented ten spaces to set them off from normal body text.

An ordered list

Indent each item in the list 10 spaces.

Follow each item with a single hard-return

One space after the period or bullet.

Do not skip extra lines before or after a list.

An unordered list

Walker 6

Unordered lists should be arranged vertically, with each item beginning on a new line.

* Dogs
* Cats
* Fish
* Birds
* Snakes

Consult your word processor's help function or manual under the topics "bullets" or "special characters" for help inserting bullets. Do not precede or follow the list with an extra line space. Place a single space after the bullet, and then begin the text.

FIGURE 6.3 List formats in printed texts.

Walker 7

In texts to be submitted for print publication, ordered lists should be preceded and followed by tags. You should enclose each item in the list with the <li> ... </li> tag pair to designate bulleted items.

        <ol>
        <li>Woke up</li>
        <li>Took a shower</li>
        <li>Went to work</li>
        <li>Ate lunch</li>
        <li>Went home</li>
        </ol>

Do not indent the list, and do not precede or follow it with an extra line space.

An ordered list in a manuscript submitted to a publisher

Walker 6

In texts to be submitted for print publication, unordered lists should be preceded and followed by tags. You may enclose each item in the list with the <li> ... </li> tag pair to designate bulleted items.

        <ul>
        <li>Dogs</li>
        <li>Cats</li>
        <li>Fish</li>
        <li>Birds</li>
        <li>Snakes</li>
        </ul>

Do not indent the items in the list or insert extra hard returns before or after the list.

An unordered list in a manuscript submitted to a publisher

FIGURE 6.4 List formats in manuscripts submitted for publication.

the assigned order. Consult your word processor's help function or manual under the topics "bullets" or "special characters" for help inserting bullets. Do not precede or follow the list with an extra line space. Place a single space after the bullet, and then begin the text. You may use your word processor's automated bulleting function if you are comfortable with it and certain that your publisher allows it, or you may chose to format unordered lists manually (see figure 6.3). In texts submitted for print publication, place a <ul> tag at the beginning of an unordered list and a </ul> tag at the end of it (see figure 6.4). Each item in the list should be enclosed with the <li> . . . </li> tag pair and flush with the left-hand margin; do not indent.

6.2.16. Quotations

6.2.16.1. Block quotations. Block quotations are quotations of roughly forty words or more that are indented more than normal body text. In professional publications, block quotations are sometimes printed in a smaller or different font from normal body text.

In print-only texts, the preferred format for block quotations is to indent the quotation ten spaces from the left margin (use your word processor's paragraph-indent capability to do this; never use the tab key or space bar for this purpose), leaving the right margin the same as it is in normal body text. The quotation should be double-spaced throughout, and you need not insert an extra line space before or after it. Block quotations should never be enclosed with quotation marks. ·

In preparing texts for print publication, begin a block quote with a <blockquote> tag, followed by a </blockquote > tag. Double-space it throughout, and do not set it off with extra line spaces or enclose it within quotation marks. Do not indent the first line of the quotation.

6.2.16.2. Epigraphs. Epigraphs are quotations placed at the very beginning of a text that somehow reflect a central idea in the text. They tend to be especially provocative or well worded.

Epigraphs should be used sparingly. In print-only texts, they should be indented ten spaces from the left margin (use your word processor's automatic paragraph-indent function to do this) and separated from the title above and the first paragraph of the text below by two hard returns. Place the author's name and the title of the excerpted work on a separate line from the quotation itself. These elements may be placed flush right or indented further.

In digital texts submitted for print publication, use the <blockquote> ... </blockquote> tag pair to format epigraphs like block quotations. The author's name and the title of the excerpted work should appear on a separate line, and the concluding </blockquote> tag should follow the title. All text should be typed flush with the left-hand margin; do not indent.

6.2.17. Note References

Numbers are sometimes placed in the body text, usually at the ends of sentences, to direct the reader to notes located at the bottoms of the pages, at the end of the document, or at the end of a subsection of the document. Corresponding numbers are placed in front of each note.

Note numbers are generally formatted in superscript, which means they hang slightly above the line on which normal body text is printed. Note numbers can be set in either eight-, nine-, or ten-point font if necessary (some word processors and printers will cut off the tops of superscript numbers unless they are reduced), or you may keep them the same size as the body text if you prefer. See section 6.1.2.3 for information on where to locate notes and how to format them.

6.2.18. Artwork

In the context of publishing, "artwork" refers to any element in a manuscript that is not textual. This includes tables, illustrations, figures, graphics, and photographs. Each individual piece of artwork should generally be stored apart from the rest of the manuscript on separate pages and as separate computer files.

Authors should be especially careful when using artwork. They should be certain that copyright has not been violated and that the artwork is appropriate and of sufficient quality to be reproduced effectively if necessary.

6.2.18.1. Tables. A table is an arrangement of words, letters, or numbers in the form of a grid or a matrix (although the lines of the grid or matrix may not be visible). Tables are designed to be read horizontally across columns and vertically down rows.

Simple tables may be created with tabs (never the space bar) to format columns and hard returns to format rows, or you may use your word processor's automatic table or columns feature if you are familiar with it and your publisher can handle it. Tables may be prepared on separate pages or placed in the interior of a manuscript, alongside normal text. When formatting tables, avoid using any formatting feature other than underlining or italics as appropriate (see section 6.2.7.2); that is, do not center or justify text; do not change fonts; do not use boldfaced type.

More complex tables need special attention. Even though increasingly more word processors offer automated functions for creating tables, authors should not use these functions to place tables in the interior of a text unless they are very comfortable with these features and publishers' guidelines specifically allow them. Instead, for manuscripts to be submitted to publishers, complex tables should be placed on separate sheets or leafs. Authors may use the automated functions of word processing or spreadsheet software to help generate such tables, but they should be stored as computer files independent from the rest of the manuscript, to be physically inserted as separate pages when the final copy is submitted. The text must make clear references to the names of any tables at the appropriate places, and each table must be labeled clearly, formatted cleanly, and printed neatly.

6.2.18.2. Illustrations. Illustrations are drawings. For texts prepared for submission to publishers, they should be placed on pages separate from the text and, if stored digitally, saved in a separate file. For all types of manuscripts, the text itself must make clear reference to each illustration at the appropriate place, and the illustrations must be labeled clearly, formatted cleanly, and printed neatly.

6.2.18.3. Figures. Figures are illustrations that include text. Graphs and charts are some of the most common figures. For works to be submitted to publishers, figures should be placed on pages separate from the text or, if stored electronically, saved in a separate file. The text itself must make clear reference to each figure at the appropriate place, and the figures must be labeled clearly, formatted cleanly, and printed neatly.

Even though increasingly more word processors offer automated functions for creating graphs and charts, authors should not use these functions to place such figures in the interior of texts intended for submission to publishers unless they are specifically allowed and then only when they have truly mastered the requirements for inserting such artwork. Authors may use the automated functions of word processing, spreadsheet, or graphics software to help generate charts or graphs, but such figures should still be stored as files independent from the rest of the manuscript, to be physically inserted as separate pages when final copy is submitted.

6.2.18.4. Graphics. Although a graphic is technically any piece of artwork, the term is most often associated with illustrations that make particular use of shading, color, and contrast for effect. Ruler lines and other minimal markings used throughout a text are also considered graphics.

Ruler lines (horizontal lines drawn across a page to enhance readability) are just about the only graphic that most authors will need to consider. Avoid using such graphics unless absolutely necessary. If you must create a ruler line in an digital text to be submitted for print publication, use either the hyphen key or the underlining key (shift-hyphen) rather than any automated word-processing function that provides ruler lines. For print-only texts, you may, of course, use the automated features provided in your word processor.

6.2.18.5. Photographs. A photograph is a picture taken with a camera. In document production, photographs often must be scanned or (re)produced into separations (of color pictures) or halftones (of black-and-white pictures) so that they will reproduce vividly on paper.

For manuscripts to be submitted to publishers, photographs should be placed on pages separate from the text or, if stored digitally, saved in a separate file. In all cases, the text itself must make clear reference to each photograph at the appropriate place, and the photographs must be labeled clearly and, if necessary, reproduced cleanly. Some photocopiers now have settings for copying photographs; use such settings if available.

Even though increasingly more word processors offer automated functions for importing images, authors preparing texts for submission to publishers should not use these functions to place photographs in the interior of a text unless they are thoroughly familiar with this feature and the publisher specifically allows it. Authors should feel welcome, however, to use technologies such as digital cameras and software that help manipulate and print photographic images, but the resulting digital photographs should still be stored as files independent from the rest of the manuscript, to be physically inserted as separate pages when final copy is submitted to publishers.

6.2.19. Style Sheets

Long before digital technologies, printers and publishers used style sheets to help define the literal mark up and appearance of the texts they produced. Most authors, before the digital age, probably approached style sheets as a list of guidelines for formatting or typesetting the various elements of a text: use four spaces to indent a new paragraph, center the author's name on the title page, print endnotes in a 10-point font. Even before the advent of the Internet, desktop publishing software was structured through style sheets: keyboarders would code a particular chunk of text as an A-level subheading or a typical body paragraph and an external style sheet, albeit now an electronic one, would determine how the various document elements would be printed. The wisdom of the style sheets is that the design or the look of the text could become external to the content of the document itself, to a large extent partitioning design issues from content and making it much easier to experiment with a variety of looks and approaches.

As the author of a print document, you may be asked to follow a publisher's style sheet for formatting your document, even if the style sheet for the final publication may be different or one you never see (e.g., the published font is almost certain to be different than the one used in the manuscript you submitted). Or you may wish to develop your own style sheet for your publication to help organize the project and manage design issues expediently. But, every contemporary author should be aware that style sheets have evolved dramatically in the information age. Online documents, like those on the Web, now rely extensively on online style sheets, which render formatting information to determine how documents will appear. Online style sheets are discussed in more detail in 7.19, but, it is important to consider that style sheets have been used widely and historically and that they have become critically important in the information age.

6.3. Submitting Documents for Print in Digital Formats

Files submitted to publishers are now most often sent either on an optical disk (CD or DVD) or online (as an email attachment or through FTP).

6.3.1. Transmitting Computer Files

If you use a disk, label the disk clearly, including the name, phone number, and email address of a person to contact in the event of problems. Be sure to write legibly on the *top* of the disk using a label or a permanent marker. Place the disk(s) in a high-quality case that will not allow the contents to move, rattle, or scratch during transfer. Label the case to correspond to the disk label(s) and package the contents securely. Do not use a chunk of cardboard and scotch tape to mail a disk. When submitting files online, organize and name the files carefully and logically (see below). Always contact the recipient to ensure all files were received and could be accessed. Double check email attachments before you send the email to ensure you attached each file intended. Large projects or large files may be too cumbersome to send or receive via email, although FTP can usually handle such transfer.

6.3.2. Naming Computer Files

Use no more than eight characters for the prefix and three characters for the file extension to ensure compatibility. Do not include spaces in the file names; instead, use the underscore character (_) if you need to designate a space. For nonanonymous submissions of work in digital form, use a version of the author's last name followed by a file extension that indicates the file format in which the text was saved (the default file extension is appropriate for most computer applications). For example, taylor.txt would be ASCII format; taylor.wpd would be *WordPerfect* 6.0 or above; taylor.doc would be used for earlier versions of *WordPerfect* files or for *Word* files; taylor.xml would be XHTML format. Using the proper file extension will allow most computer applications to recognize the type of file automatically and translate it accurately.

If multiple files are submitted (including illustrations, figures, and so on, or for multiple sections or chapters saved as separate files), number the files sequentially and indicate the file format. For example, tay_fig1.jpg (figure 1 of the Taylor manuscript, in **JPEG** format), tay_fig2.png (figure 2 of the Taylor manuscript, in PNG format), tay_ch1.txt (chapter 1 of the Taylor manuscript, in ASCII format), or tay_ch2.wpd (chapter 2 of the Taylor manuscript, in *WordPerfect* 12.0 format).

If different parts of a manuscript are saved as separate files, file names should reflect both the author's name and the name of the individual element. For example, tay_pre.txt (preface of the Taylor manuscript, in ASCII format) or tay_toc.doc (table of contents of the Taylor manuscript, in Word format). For a complex manuscript submission with many files, disks or attachments should be accompanied by a written, annotated explanation of the contents and format of each file. For smaller submissions, list the file names and each file's type on the disk label or in the attached email.

If the name of the author must be kept anonymous for review purposes, follow the principles outlined above, only substitute the first important word (or a truncated version) of the title for the author's name. For example, if an article entitled "The Changing Internet" were being submitted, it should be named changing.txt, changing.wpd, changing.doc, or changing.xml (as appropriate), and auxiliary files of the article or manuscript should be titled cha_fig1.jpg or cha_fig2.png or the like.

7

CREATING DOCUMENTS
FOR ELECTRONIC PUBLICATION

This chapter presents effective standards and guidelines for authors, editors, and publishers who wish to create digital documents that are easily transferable from one application or platform to another, especially if these texts are to be published on computer networks, such as the WWW. Authors whose work will be published on a computer network should follow the standards described in this chapter. This chapter is not intended to itemize all the ins and outs of markup languages; for that, you should buy one of the many guides already in print or visit W3C's HTML tutorial at http://www.w3schools.com/html/default.asp as a place to start.

The logic of computer networks can contribute immensely to developing standards for the format of academic documents online (and in print). In order for computer files to be exchanged across platforms and applications, these files must be prepared using generic formats so that a variety of people using a variety of computer equipment and software can gain access. As a result, highly uniform format standards, such as XHTML, have emerged.

As with documents intended for print formats, however, a cardinal rule governs working with documents intended for electronic publication: *In all circumstances, keep it simple.*

The guidelines in this chapter are intended to prevent the unique logic of a word processor from interfering with the easy portability of files to a network. Many authors of academic texts are likely to use a word-processing program to compose and format documents for digital publication. Many of the newer versions of most word processors allow for automatic translation of standard word-processing codes into HTML, XML, and PDF format. Translating many of the automatic formatting features of a word processor can still cause problems, however, so avoid using these features (such as the automatic paragraph indent or automatic footnoting features) if possible. If you are using the automatic HTML/XML publishing feature of a word processor, avoid including hypertextual tags (i.e., tags enclosed in **angle brackets**) in the text: angle brackets are reserved characters in hypertext, yet most word processors will automatically translate them into hyperlinks rather than retaining them as hypertext commands. Instead, you will need to add these commands to the hypertext using an ASCII text editor or HTML editor in order to format your document adequately. Use a Web browser to verify that any documents you translate from a word processor to HTML format have been formatted properly, and use the WC3's online XML Validator Service to check XML code (http://validator.w3.org).

The cardinal rule of online document design has four important corollaries:

Corollary 1: Do not use any of your text editor's formatting features unless you absolutely must. Do not change fonts, do not change margins, do not use fancy fonts, do not center or fully justify text, do not use blinking text unless you absolutely must in order to meet the demands of your intended audience.

Corollary 2: Do not invent new elements of document style unless you absolutely must. Almost all professional academic authors will need only two special formatting features to produce an online text: italics (not underlining) and hypertextual links (see section 7.2.3). Authors who wish to use footnotes or endnotes should consider using hypertextual links. Authors working online must also abjure hanging indentation for bibliographic entries because most XHTML documents do not readily lend themselves to this formatting. All authors should, however, take advantage of text-editor functions such as spell checkers, used wisely but not as a substitute for careful proofreading.

Corollary 3: Use logical tags, not typographical formatting, to denote the various elements of document style. These tags can be easily replaced by either traditional word-processing commands or XHTML tags, as necessary. See the discussion under corollary 3 in chapter 6 for an explanation of the logic behind these formatting codes.

Corollary 4: The original-content document should be formatted using logical tags, but the material appearance for the document is best determined by a second, exterior document called a "style sheet." Academic authors need only to format or tag their documents using XHTML. In general and for the purposes of the standards in this book, they can leave the responsibility for corresponding style sheets to their publisher. However, if authors wish to self-publish online, they will need to consult section 7.2.19 to learn about creating rudimentary style sheets.

Keeping the cardinal rule of document design for networked texts and its four corollaries in mind can solve a great many problems for authors, editors, and publishers; however, specific ramifications of these rules need to be spelled out. Table 7.1 summarizes the general rules to follow when preparing a document for electronic publication. More detailed explanations and rules for the individual components of document style follow.

TABLE 7.1 Preparing a Document for Electronic Publication

- Use metatags to identify authors, contributors, titles, and necessary publication information.

- Be aware that some formatting features will not be readable by all Web browsers; you should therefore try to use only the basic formatting features and codes described in this chapter unless you are required to do otherwise.

- Avoid using underlining for most purposes; use italics instead.

- Use boldface sparingly—for instance, when required in certain mathematical formulas

- Use the paragraphs tags (<p> and </p>) to separate sections and paragraphs to be preceded and followed by extra line space. See section 7.2.14 for a discussion of these tags.

- Do not use the space bar or tab key to indent. Paragraphs should be set off with the paragraph tags; they need not be indented. Block quotations, lists, and other elements that may require indenting in final electronically published form should be set off using the proper XHTML tags (e.g., <blockquote> . . . </blockquote>, <ol> . . . </ol>, and <ul> . . . </ul>).

- In most instances, allow lines to wrap automatically; do not try to force features of print texts, such as double spacing and hanging indents, into electronic formats, as these features may create difficulty for some readers using different hardware and software applications.

- Use table codes to create simple tables.

- Do not center or right-justify text unless required to do so. If you must center some portions of your text, use the appropriate alignment tag pair.

- For most academic texts, keep your design relatively austere. These texts need to be especially portable and readable, and advanced formatting codes and applications (such as large graphics files or audio and video files requiring plug-ins or special browsers) may prevent many readers with limited technological capabilities from accessing your work.

TABLE 7.1 Preparing a Document for Electronic Publication (*continued*)

> • Format your documents carefully to save potential readers, compilers, and editors anguish. Each online document should contain a byline and a title (see sections 7.2.9 and 7.2.10). If your document contains multiple files, it should contain a title or contents page to which all other pages in the work refer (see sections 7.1.1.2 and 7.1.1.5).

7.1. THE PARTS OF THE TEXT

7.1.1. Front Matter

See section 6.1.1. Front matter of chapter- and article-length texts may be stored in the same file and at the same URL as the body text; however, the author may want to use page anchor tags (see section 7.2.2) to allow navigation around the various elements of the text. Each element of front matter for longer projects should be stored in a separate computer file, located at a unique URL. In such cases, authors should provide navigational links to identify and access such information.

Authors working in XHTML/SGML or other similar formats should use metatags on each separate file. Metatags are hypertext tags within the <head> . . . </head> tag pair of an XHTML file that provide information about the document, such as the author's name, the creation date, the title, and a description of the document. This information can then be sought using search engines designed for the purpose; it can also be accessed by viewing the file's XHTML source code. For example, the following code will allow the information contained in it to be viewed in the source code and indexed by search engines and other programs that search for specific information online:

> <META NAME = "Author" CONTENT = "Todd Taylor">
> <META NAME = "Creation Date" CONTENT = "21 Jun. 2006
> 15:54 GMT">
> <META NAME = "Title" CONTENT = "Metatags">
> <META NAME = "Abstract" CONTENT = "Examples of the
> use of metatags to provide bibliographic information in
> hypertext documents">

Metatags can also contain other information, such as keywords chosen by the author to facilitate searches. Many XHTML editing programs will automatically include some of this information.

The following elements are discussed in the order in which they usually appear in texts.

7.1.1.1. *Covers and cover pages.* Material relating to the cover, if applicable, should be stored in a separate file and at a different URL from the rest of the publication, often the index.xml page (see section 7.2.1). Covers for online publications should contain obvious links to the rest of the text.

A cover page is a single page that contains at least the complete title of the work and the name(s) and affiliation(s) of the work's author(s), editor(s), and translator(s). Articles, essays, and chapters do not necessarily require cover pages; the title, the authors' names and affiliations, and the date of publication can be placed on the first page of the text instead. If used, however, the cover page should be located at a discrete URL and should thus contain an obvious link (or links) to the rest of the text.

7.1.1.2. *Title page.* See section 6.1.1.2. The title page should also list the URL of publication and may include the email addresses of the author(s) or editor(s) and the publication date. Other appropriate information (such as any special software applications necessary to access the text adequately) may also be included.

7.1.1.3. Information page. See section 6.1.1.3. Note that the appropriateness of including some of this information online is questionable.

7.1.1.4. Abstract or summary. See section 6.1.1.4. When formatting an abstract, locate it either immediately after the title of the publication or at a separate URL. Head it with the word "Abstract" enclosed within the <h2> ... </h2> tag pair to designate it as a chapter head (see section 6.2.10.1). Note: In hypertext documents, it is unnecessary to center titles or subheads.

7.1.1.5. Table of contents. The table of contents is a list of the major divisions, sections, or chapters of a book-length manuscript. Because page numbers are irrelevant online, the contents should use hypertextual links rather than page numbers to key the names of the major divisions to the relevant subsections (see section 7.2.3). Head the contents with the words "Table of Contents" (or "Contents") coded as a chapter head (i.e., enclosed within the <h2> ... </h2> tag pair; see section 6.2.10.1).

7.1.1.6. List of illustrations and figures. See section 6.1.1.6. Because page numbers are irrelevant online, the list may contain hypertextual links between the items noted and the corresponding artwork rather than page numbers (see section 7.2.3). Code the title of the page or section as a chapter head by enclosing it within the <h2> ... </h2> tag pair (see section 6.2.10.1).

7.1.1.7. List of tables. See section 6.1.1.7. Each title in such a list should be a hypertextual link to the appropriate table or page online (see section 7.2.3). Code the title of the page or section as a chapter head by enclosing it within the <h2> ... </h2> tag pair (see section 6.2.10.1).

7.1.1.8. Foreword. See section 6.1.1.8. In a longer text, the foreword should be placed in a separate file with a unique URL. Code the title of the page or section as a chapter head by enclosing it within the <h2> . . . </h2> tag pair (see section 6.2.10.1).

7.1.1.9. Acknowledgments. See section 6.1.1.9. In a longer text, the acknowledgments should be placed in a separate file with a unique URL, unless they are included in the preface, which is often the case. Code the title of the page or section as a chapter head by enclosing it within the <h2> . . . </h2> tag pair (see section 6.2.10.1).

7.1.1.10. Preface. A preface is a commentary written by the author(s) that discusses the project that follows. Prefaces typically address information about the publication of the text, such as the history of the project, important contributors, or editions or translations of the text; such information may also be handled through an author's or editor's note.

When formatting a preface for a book-length electronic publication, head the text with the word "Preface" coded as a chapter head (i.e., enclosed within the <h2> . . . </h2> tag pair; see section 6.2.10.1). When including a preface in an article-length text, format its title as an A-level subhead (see section 6.2.13); do not place the preface on a separate page from the material that follows, unless it is longer than two thousand words.

7.1.1.11. Introduction. An introduction is commentary written by the author(s) that discusses the project that follows. Unlike a preface, introductions typically orient the reader to the ensuing text's argument or content, usually including substantial information about the organization and theme of the text. However, no hard and fast rule can be said to distinguish clearly the function of a preface from that of an introduction. It is highly unlikely that an article will require both a preface and an introduction, although this is not uncommon in book-length works.

When formatting an introduction for a publication, locate it immediately before the body of the text, but do not place it on a separate page unless it is longer than about two thousand words. In a book-length text, title it with the word "Introduction" coded as a chapter head with the <h2> ... </h2> tag pair (see section 6.2.10.1); in an article-length text, format the title as an A-level subhead (see section 6.2.13).

7.1.2. Back Matter

See section 6.1.2. Whenever placing an item of back matter at a separate URL instead of at the same URL as the body text, authors must provide navigational links to identify and access such information.

7.1.2.1. Conclusion. A conclusion is a commentary written by the author(s) or editor(s) that discusses the preceding text. Conclusions serve various purposes, among them summarizing and synthesizing important points of the material, emphasizing certain points for effect, providing a structural capstone to the text, driving home a particular point, or establishing extensions and generalizations for further consideration based upon the present document.

When formatting a conclusion for electronic publication, locate it after all other body matter but before all other back matter. Do not isolate the conclusion on a separate page, unless it is longer than about two thousand words. In a book-length text, title it with the word "Conclusion" coded as a chapter head with the <h2> ... </h2> tag pair (see section 6.2.10.1); in an article-length text, format the title as an A-level subhead (see section 6.2.13).

7.1.2.2. Appendixes. See section 6.1.2.2. Follow the guidelines for artwork in section 7.2.18, including all the subsections there, for appendixes containing tables and other artwork.

7.1.2.3. Notes. Notes are itemized ancillary commentary on isolated ideas or assertions in the body text. Notes are generally numbered in order to correspond to references—usually numerical super-scripts—located at the relevant places in the body text. Locate the notes themselves at the end of the document, before the bibliography, and entitle them with the word "Notes" coded as a chapter head with the <h2> ... </h2> tag pair (see section 6.2.10.1). Super-script note references are often difficult to read online, thus, use hypertextual links instead to connect paraphrasings or quotations to their sources, in which case you may choose to locate the notes at a separate URL (see section 7.2.3). Hypertextual links between citations in the body text itself and the bibliography can also be highly effective. However, most academic hypertext should follow traditional parenthetical citation formats. Even there, though, references to other online sources should also be linked to the original source if possible. For a more complete discussion of in-text citations, see part 1.

7.1.2.4. Glossary. A glossary is an alphabetical listing of important terms used in the text. For hypertext glossaries, enclose the entire list within the <dl> ... </dl> tag pair; enclose each term with the <dt> ... </dt> tag pair and each definition with the <dd> ... </dd> tag pair. Code the title of the page or section (i.e., "Glossary") as a chapter head using the <h2> ... </h2> tag pair (see section 6.2.10.1). Creating hypertextual links between in-text terms and glossary entries is an especially effective way to format a glossary (see section 7.2.3).

7.1.2.5. Bibliography. A bibliography is a list of information regarding works that were referenced in the creation of a manuscript. Because hypertext links do not necessarily show the URL when they are printed out, for now the bibliography is a necessity in any text—especially an academic text—that refers to outside sources, even if all those sources are located online.

Forms and structures for organizing bibliographies vary significantly; however, the entries are almost always arranged alphabetically according to the last names of the cited author(s) or editor(s) or the first major word in the title of the work being cited if no author or editor name is available. A bibliographic listing of the works directly referenced in a text is typically titled "Works Cited" or "References." Resources that were consulted but not cited while producing the manuscript are sometimes listed in a separate bibliography entitled "Works Consulted." Whatever the title chosen, code it as a chapter head by enclosing it within the <h2> . . . </h2> tag pair (see section 6.2.10.1).

The bibliography should be located at the end of a document. Surround each entry in a bibliography with paragraph tags (<p> and </p>; see section 7.2.14) so it will be followed by white space. No indentation is necessary. You may also arrange an online bibliography as an unordered list. Place the <ul> tag in front of the entire bibliography and the </ul> tag at the end. Place an <li> tag (used to code a bulleted list) in front of each entry (see section 7.2.15, as well as figure 7.1, which provides an example of a bulleted list used for a bibliography) or use the <p> . . . </p> tag pair instead (this will prevent bullets from appearing in front of each item and separate each entry from the next with white space). Do *not* try to form hanging indents online as this may interfere with the automatic word-wrap feature in most browsers and cause difficulty for the reader.

- ESPN Radio Daily. "Favre Mulls Retirement." 30 Jan. 2006. ESPN Radio Podcast. http://sports.espn.go.com/espn/news/story?id=2092153 (31 Jan. 2006).

- True, Alice L. "Academic Literacy in a Wired World: Redefining Genres for College Writing Courses." *Kairos: Rhetoric, Technology, Pedagogy* 7.2 (2002). http://english.ttu.edu/kairos/ (7 June 2006).

FIGURE 7.1 An example of a bulleted list used for references.

If you make use of hypertextual links (see section 7.2.3), you can place the bibliography at a separate URL. Hypertextual links between citations in the body text itself and a bibliography can be highly effective. (For example, in figure 7.2 the underlined references in the text point to the reference in the bibliography, and the entry in the bibliography in figure 7.1 points to the source itself.) Parenthetical references will still be necessary, however, for most academic texts. Full URLs should be listed for each online source, as well, even if an entry is already linked to its source; this will ensure that readers will be able to obtain access to the sources even if they are unable to follow the links (as may occur if the hypertext has been printed out).

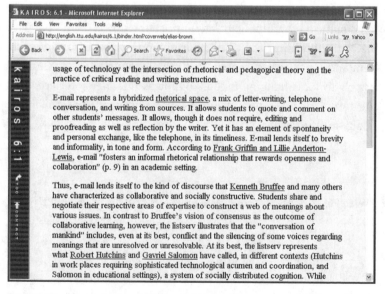

FIGURE 7.2 An example of in-text references in hypertext.

Source: http://english.ttu.edu/kairos/6.1/binder.html?coverweb/elias=brown

7.1.2.6. Index. An index is an alphabetical listing of topics, names, or titles discussed in the text. Because page numbers do not really exist in online documents, indexes should use hypertextual links between entries in the index and the referenced text (see section 7.2.3). However, because each entry may need to link to more than one location, online indexes may be very difficult to format. Moreover, because digital text can be more easily searched than print text, indexes may be less necessary. Even so, a list of key terms with links to the corresponding chapters or URLs discussing such terms can be helpful to readers. Once inside a particular URL, a reader can search for the indexed word itself. If an indexed word is a common term or appears repeatedly throughout a text, authors can cite it as part of the relevant phrase in which it appears in the body text so that readers can search for the reference more precisely.

If included, the index page should be headed with the word "Index" coded as a chapter head using the <h2> ... </h2> tag pair (see section 6.2.10.1). Index entries may be formatted by placing a <ul> or <ol> tag after the head, before the first list item, and a </ul> or </ol> tag after the last item and surrounding each item by the <p> ... </p> tags (for an unbulleted list) or the <li> ... </li> tags (for a bulleted list) as desired. If you have the necessary know-how and online resources, you might also consider installing a searchable index (an interactive feature that allows users to search a specific site for keywords or terms).

7.1.2.7. List of contributors. The list of contributors presents brief biographical information about the authors who contributed to a text. Italicize each author's name, or code it as an email link to the author's email address, if desired, using the <a href = " "> ... </a> tag pair. Enclose each entry in the list within the <p> ... </p> tag pair (see section 7.2.14). Creating two-way hypertextual links between bylines and the entries on the contributors can be an especially effective way to format these lists (see section 7.2.3).

7.2. PUBLISHING DOCUMENTS ON A COMPUTER NETWORK

7.2.1. File Organization

Locate all files relating to a particular document in the same directory, if possible, and, again if possible, include only files relating to the document in that directory. The cover page or opening page of the site, if applicable, should be named index.xml, if possible, so that it will be the default page for the site or directory. For example, http://www.unc.edu/~twtaylor will automatically open up the file at http://www.unc.edu/~twtaylor/index.xml unless another file name is specified. All files may be saved in the default directory (~twtaylor in this example) or in subdirectories created within the root directory. Links from the main page will allow readers easy access without long URLs.

7.2.2. Navigating and Frames

Since page numbers are irrelevant (or nonexistent) online, authors must use a system that allows readers to navigate through their texts effectively. Shorter texts may use page anchors as navigation aids (see figure 7.3). Longer texts should separate large segments of text into discrete computer files with unique URLs, and create navigational links between the URLs. Any segment of text much larger than two thousand words (or even fewer for WWW documents) should be formatted with a structure that permits effective navigation. Two common approaches to navigation are (1) to place hypertextual links either at the beginning of a file or at the end (see section 7.2.3) and (2) to use frames.

Authors should be aware that many readers will have difficulty using frames effectively unless they have access to frames-compatible browsers. Many sites that use frames thus offer a nonframes version as well. Nevertheless, frames can be an effective navigational aid if used carefully.

7.2.3. Links

Create hypertextual links when appropriate by surrounding the text you wish to serve as a link (or hot spot) with the tag pair <a href = " ">...</a>. This will create a link between the text and the referenced URL and will usually change the font color of the linked text to blue and underline it (in most browser settings). Make sure that the text you choose to serve as a link is sufficiently explanatory of where the link will take the reader and as brief as possible (a page with too many long links can be difficult to read). Consider, too, that URLs outside your control may disappear over time; if necessary, you may want to include (as an appendix) a list of the external links used in your work, including a brief discussion of what was at the linked URL at the time. Each separate page of your own site should include a link back to either the cover page or the contents page and may also contain links to other parts of the document, if appropriate. An author should confirm that all links in a text are functioning properly (that is, a click on each highlighted term actually connects the reader to the appropriate site) before submitting or publishing an online text.

7.2.4. Colors

If you feel background colors or textures or font colors other than black are integral to your publication, you may use them, but do so with extreme caution: they tend to be distracting and may decrease readability if overused. Reading onscreen is already more difficult than reading printed material, so anything that reduces the contrast between text and the background should be avoided. For this reason, it is best not to format text with color. If you are using colored fonts or backgrounds, however, you may also want to consider changing the default colors for linked text to avoid clashing. (See chapter 6 for a more detailed discussion of the pros and cons of color in academic documents.)

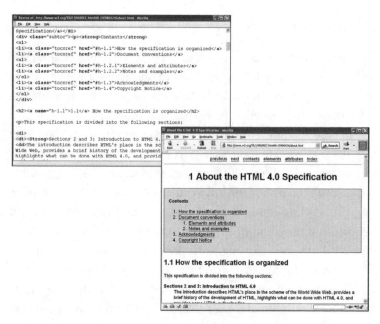

FIGURE 7.3 Using page anchors.

Source: http://www.w3.org/TR/1988/REC=html140=19980424/about.html

7.2.5. Spacing

Do not attempt to double-space text in online documents; this may be difficult to do and may cause more problems than it solves. Auto-wrap features enable text to fit within browser windows, regardless of what size window the user may select. Forcing extra spacing may defeat this and actually make the text harder to read onscreen. Even hard-copy printouts may be adversely affected unless the hypertext author attempts to ensure that the text will fit on standard size paper (keeping in mind that U.S. and European paper standards differ), a task that can be most arduous given the many different printer programs, software defaults, and user changes.

7.2.6. Fonts

Use default fonts unless you absolutely must do otherwise; do not add color or a specific font face or size unless you must. In fact, the XHTML standard requires that font definitions be located in a corresponding style sheet. Use only the header tag pairs—<h1> . . . </h1>, <h2> . . . </h2>, <h3> . . . </h3>, and so on—to indicate titles and subheads (see sections 6.2.13, 7.2.10, and 7.2.13). Allow body text to remain at default settings if possible. Readers often can override the fonts, font sizes, and font colors selected by an author, so any choices you make may not appear on the reader's screen.

7.2.7. Formatting Techniques

7.2.7.1. Boldface. See section 6.2.7.1. An author can format text in boldface online by enclosing it within the <b> . . . </b> tag pair. Use boldface sparingly and only when absolutely necessary. It should not be used to indicate emphasis.

7.2.7.2. Underlining and italics. Underlining is a formatting technique used online to designate a hypertextual link and should be reserved for this purpose in all but exceptional circumstances. There is no need to insert special codes to underline hypertext links for most WWW documents; the <a href = " "> . . . </a> tag pair will usually automatically format linked text. The <u> . . . </u> tag pair is now obsolete and should not be used.

While italics are the preferred means to indicate emphasis, titles of large works (such as books, movies, etc.), foreign words, terminology, and other elements that are sometimes underlined in print texts, these elements should not be formatted identically online. Titles of large works should use the <cite> . . . </cite> tag pair; terminology, including foreign words, should use the <dfn> . . . </dfn> tag pair; normal emphasis is accomplished with the <em> . . .

</em> pair; and strong emphasis uses the <strong> . . . </strong> pair. HTML has a tag to include blinking text for added emphasis, but blinking text is inappropriate in academic writing. In all other cases, use the <i> . . . </i> tag pair to create italicized text. (See the discussion in section 6.2.7.2 for details.)

For ASCII text editors, email programs, and text-only browsers, such as **Lynx**, that do not recognize either italics or underlining, we recommend using the underscore character (_) before and after the text, for example, _The Columbia Guide to Online Style_.

Most of the other tags discussed above are also unreadable in text-only versions, so, to indicate emphasis in such formats, many users place asterisks (*) around the text they wish to emphasize, for example, *This text is emphasized*. Asterisks are also sometimes used, especially in email messages, to indicate "emotes," or facial expressions, as in *grin*. Some ASCII authors may also surround text with emotes enclosed in angle brackets, thus allowing a mixture of face-to-face and print elements. For example: <smile>It's later than you think</smile>. And, of course, we have all seen :-), the sideways smiley face called an emoticon.

7.2.8. Special Characters

See section 6.2.8. To insert a special character in your text, you may use the appropriate ISO number set, preceded by "&#" and followed immediately by a semicolon. For example, "©" will appear as the copyright symbol © when viewed through a Web browser. You may also use the XHTML character set for reserved characters (for example, "<" is the symbol for the left angle bracket, <).

7.2.9. Bylines

A byline indicates the author(s) of the work and other relevant information such as affiliation or geographic location. It should be placed at the very beginning of each document, on the title page if appropriate. Using the standard default font, list each author's first name followed by the middle initial and surname. On a separate line or lines include other relevant information such as date, and institutional affiliation. Use the <p> ... </p> tag pair to separate items in the byline. Do not include a byline when submitting work for anonymous grading or review. (See also metatags in section 7.1.1.)

7.2.10. Titles

See section 6.2.10. Titles of documents placed online also serve the important function of giving the document an identity to be referenced by those using search engines. Enclose the full title of a Web site or a larger online work within the <title> ... </title> tag pair in the head of each separate page that is part of the complete document, including any other relevant information (such as chapter number or title) as appropriate. This title may be repeated on each page by enclosing it within the <h1> ... </h1> tag pair in the body of the document. Chapter and section titles should then be enclosed within the <h2> ... </h2> tag pair, if applicable (see also sections 7.2.10.1 and 7.2.10.2).

7.2.10.1. Titles for article- or chapter-length projects. Place the article or chapter title immediately before the byline, enclosed within the <h2> ... </h2> tag pair (see section 6.2.10.1). Do not use all capital letters for titles, and it is not necessary to boldface, underline, or italicize them. For article-or chapter-length projects, the full title and the article or chapter title may be the same.

7.2.10.2. Titles for book-length projects. In the case of book-length projects that consist of several online files, the title of the complete work should be included in the XHTML head, enclosed within the <title> ... </title> tag pair and should be repeated immediately before the byline, enclosed within the <h1> ... </h1> tag pair.

7.2.11. Section Numbers

Section numbers, which provide a constant and sequential system for referencing specific locations in a text, can be inserted in online texts if they will help readers locate information more easily. Hypertextual page anchors can serve similar purposes (see section 7.2.3). Section numbers may be manually inserted, or you may choose to format the sections using the <ol> ... </ol> tag pair, enclosing each numbered section within the <li> ... </li> tag pair.

7.2.12. Return Links

As a courtesy to your readers, include a return link and any other navigational links on every URL within your site. Return links are typically placed either at the bottom of a page or in a frame. If your document features a contents page, provide a link back to it. If your document does not have a linear organization, include a link back to your title page. A link taking readers back to the previous node, or page, is helpful in linear texts as well. Links to major divisions within a text are helpful but not essential.

7.2.13. Subheads

See section 6.2.13. For online subheads, use upper- and lowercase letters, not all capitals. Do not use boldface, italics, or underlining to format subheads unless it is absolutely necessary; instead, use the tag pairs listed in section 6.2.13.

7.2.14. Paragraphs

See section 6.2.14. To indicate paragraphs online, place a <p> tag at the beginning of each new paragraph and a </p> tag at the end of each paragraph. It is unnecessary to indent paragraphs in online documents.

7.2.15. Lists

7.2.15.1. Ordered lists. See section 6.2.15.1, especially the discussion of how to format ordered lists in texts that will be submitted electronically for print publication. Ordered lists in online documents may also be "nested," that is, you may open multiple ordered lists within other lists to create an indented list similar in structure to an outline. With XHTML, you must take great care to ensure tags are nested perfectly, and you can use WC3's online XML Validator Service to check XML code (http://validator.w3.org).

7.2.15.2. Unordered lists. See section 6.2.15.2, especially the discussion of how to format unordered lists in both print and electronic form. As with ordered lists, unordered lists may be nested to create an indented listing. With XHTML, you must take great care to ensure tags are nested perfectly, and you can use WC3's online XML Validator Service to check XML code (http://validator.w3.org).

7.2.16. Quotations

7.2.16.1. Block quotations. See section 6.2.16.1, particularly the discussion of how to format block quotations in texts prepared digitally for submission for print publication. Do not change fonts for block quotations online.

7.2.16.2. Epigraphs. See section 6.2.16.2, particularly the discussion of how to format epigraphs in texts submitted in electronic form for print publication. An epigraph will be distinguishable from a block quotation by its positioning at the very front of a text and by the inclusion of the author's name and the source title.

7.2.17. Note References

See section 6.2.17. Note numbers in online documents can be placed in superscript by using the ^{. . .} tag pair. However, a more dynamic approach would be to create a hypertextual link between body text and notes placed elsewhere in the document. See sections 7.1.2.3 and 7.2.3.

7.2.18. Artwork

See section 6.2.18. Artwork for online publications will almost always be stored in computer files separate from the body text, with each piece located within the text by means of the <img src = " " /> tag, which places artwork stored at a separate URL as a graphic file on the page at the indicated location. You may define the parameters of the image file within the <img src = " " /> tag by including other XHTML codes, such as the "alt" attribute (which assigns a description name to graphic files for readers without graphical browsers) or the "height" and "width" commands (which allow the author to specify the number of pixels the graphic image will encompass). However, you should always use the "alt = " attribute as an essential courtesy to your readers, especially those who may be visually impaired. For example, <img src = "http://www.unc.edu/graphics/seal.png" alt = "The University of North Carolina seal" height = 220 width = 220 /> is a tag used to place the image file "seal.png" in a Web page. Note that XHTML standard requires a single space and a slash at the end of the <img src = " " /> tag.

Authors must make sure that graphics files are scaled to use as little computer memory as possible. Avoid images larger than 25K (10K and below is preferable), and do not allow a single URL to include more than 200K of artwork. Authors may align artwork flush left, center, or flush right; but flush left is the default. JPEG and PNG file formats are currently the standard for artwork published online.

7.2.18.1. Tables. See section 6.2.18.1. Most tables can be effectively composed online using the table functions supported by HTML. Avoid using unnecessary formatting features—i.e., centering or justifying text, changing fonts, and using boldface, italics, or underlining—unless absolutely necessary. More complex tables, however, require special attention. These may be produced in print, digitized using a scanner, and inserted as JPEG or PNG files when necessary. Use tables with caution, however, because text-only browsers such as Lynx do not recognize table codes and can make information contained within <table> ... </table> tag pairs difficult to read. And, with XHTML, you must take great care to ensure table tags are nested perfectly. You can use WC3's online XML Validator Service to check XML code (http://validator.w3.org).

7.2.18.2. Illustrations.

See section 6.2.18.2.

7.2.18.3. Figures.

See section 6.2.18.3.

7.2.18.4. Graphics. See section 6.2.18.4. In addition to adding graphics in JPEG or PNG formats, authors of online documents can create simple horizontal lines to enhance readability by using the <hr> ... </hr> tag pair. The length and width of the <hr> tag can also be defined by inserting the appropriate codes within the angle brackets (for instance, <hr size = 2 width = 500 align = center> ... </hr> will create a horizontal rule centered on a page extending 500 pixels across the page and 2 pixels thick. Icons, buttons, image maps (graphics with certain areas defined as links to discrete URLs), and other graphics used for navigational purposes online may be helpful when used appropriately; however, keep graphics simple and functional. Animated bullets and blinking text are unnecessary for most academic documents and can be extremely distracting to readers.

7.2.18.5. Photographs. See section 6.2.18.5. Photographs must first be digitized in order to be displayed online. Reducing photographs from 256 or more colors to 16 colors when digitizing is a particularly effective means of reducing file sizes for most online applications. Cropping pictures to exclude extraneous backgrounds can also be helpful. It is better to size graphics using a program designed to work with digitized images to fit the desired space on the Web page instead of using the "height" and "width" attributes in the <img src = " " /> tag, because these attributes do not reduce the file size and can cause considerable distortions of some images.

7.2.19. Style Sheets

One of the tremendous advantages of the emergence of standards for online document style is the (significant) separation of content from design. Ideally, an online document should be formatted or tagged in a purely logical way, with no actual definition of design and appearance. Instead, the design and appearance of the document are left to an external document, called a style sheet. For example, the content file indicates that a certain chunk of text is a second-level subheading and that a different chunk of text is a standard body paragraph. But, the literal appearance or rendering (of the corresponding font face, size, shape, color, spacing, etc.) for these elements is determined by an external style sheet. Most early HTML documents did not rely, in practice, on style sheets, although SGML, the parent of HTML, encouraged such use. Many of these early online documents were self-contained, meaning that literal, material, and spatial design issues were coded directly into the HTML document. However, publishers of large quantities of online material realized that embedding design parameters into content documents created great difficulty as the need to modify, maintain, and update the original material emerged. If your corporate font became unfashionable, as fonts do, or new Web browsers began to render differently embedded elements, as browsers do, someone had to undergo the tedious and expensive task of figuring out how to recode or reformat potentially thousands of individual documents—violating most of the principles of document design described in chapter 6. Consequently, design standards for online documents returned to the spirit of SGML by reinstitutionalizing style sheets.

One of the defining characteristics of the new XHTML/XML standard is that each content document should refer to a second, corresponding style sheet. On the one hand, the additional responsibility of properly compiling this second document will no doubt dissuade many academic authors for moving from previous standards to XHTML/XML. Indeed, the choices and technological knowledge involved in enabling authors to wield anything beyond the most rudimentary XML documents and corresponding style sheets is beyond the scope of this book. On the other hand, most academic authors can merely tag or format their content document according to the guidelines in this chapter and leave the design and style sheet responsibilities to others anyway—which may be the best approach for most authors in the long run, even when authors are adept at creating online style sheets. However, if needed, authors can use the simple code for a rudimentary style sheet in figure 7.4 as a companion to their XML document. Note that authors can use the sample style sheet for a multitude of content files that refer to it, which is the beauty of style sheets; namely, you can modify the design of an ocean of documents by only modifying the one style sheet to which each of the documents refers. Also note that, thus, your content document must contain code (also included in figure 7.4) in order to locate, connect to, and employ its corresponding style sheet. But again, for the purposes of

```
<stylesheet version="1.0"
xmlns="http://www.w3.org/1999/XSL/Transform">
    <template match="/">
        <copy-of select="." />
    </template>
</stylesheet>
```

- Locate the exact code above in a text file named "mystyle.xsl".
- Save this file in the same directory as your content file.

```
<?xml version="1.0"?>
<?xml-stylesheet type="text/xsl" href="style.xsl"?>
<html>

[paste your content between the <html>...</html> tags]

</html>
```

- Locate the exact code above in your content file.
- Be sure the file begins with the three first lines.
- Be sure the file ends with the last line, closing the html tag pair.
- Code your XML document very precisely, and validate the code.
- Save the file as a text file, with the *.xml extension.
- Save this file in the same directory as the "mystyle.xsl" stylesheet.

FIGURE 7.4 Sample style sheet template.

this book, an author need only tag/format the original document properly and leave style sheet responsibility to someone else.

7.3. SUBMITTING FILES FOR ELECTRONIC PUBLICATION

7.3.1. Diskettes and CDs

See section 6.3.1.

7.3.2. Naming Computer Files

See section 6.3.2. Note that files submitted to an editor or publisher of online documents exchanged through a network may use larger file names and extensions (for instance, "englishpages.html" is an acceptable file name online but not for most **DOS** applications). Names of files to be exchanged on disk or email attachment, however, should have file names of no more than eight characters and file extensions of no more than three characters to allow for portability across platforms.

Appendix A

STARTING POINTS FOR INTERNET RESEARCH

LIBRARY CATALOGS

The Australian National Library (http://www.nla.gov.au).
   A searchable index of the national Library of Australia Web site, including a link to the National Library of Australia's Online Public Access Catalogue.

Internet Public Library (http://www.ipl.org).
   The Internet Public Library offers an online ready-reference collection, a searchable database, links to over 20,000 books, and reference librarians to answer individual questions.

Library of Congress (http://lcweb.loc.gov/homepage/lchp.html).
   A searchable index to sources available from the Library of Congress home page.

LibWeb (http://sunsite.berkeley.edu/Libweb).
   Berkeley Digital Library's list of library servers available on the World Wide Web.

Library and Archives Canada (http://www.nlc-bnc.ca/ehome.htm). Available in both French and English, Library and Archives Canada is designed to provide easy access to texts, photographs, and other documents relating to Canada and Canadians.

Networked Digital Library of Theses and Dissertations (NDLTD) (http://www.theses.org). Collections of theses and dissertations available in electronic formats as part of an initiative at a growing number of institutions to require that all theses and dissertations be published electronically and freely available.

WWW Virtual Library (http://www.vlib.org). A searchable list of subject-specific links to World Wide Web resources.

Yahoo!'s List of Library Links (http://www.yahoo.com/Reference/ Libraries). Links to libraries sorted by content area, including lists of academic libraries; music, literature, art, and Native American resources; and maps, special collections, and much more. Many of the libraries offer searchable indexes or online sources.

SELECTED GENERAL AND MULTIDISCIPLINARY DATABASES

Check with your library for how to access subscriber databases.

Academic Search Premier

Abstracts, including many that are full text or full image, and indexing for more than 3,000 scholarly journals and general magazines on a variety of topics.

ArticleFirst

Bibliographic citations for articles in over 12,000 scholarly journals of science, technology, medicine, social science, business, the humanities, and popular culture.

EBSCO

A major publisher of full-text and bibliographic databases that can be searched either individually or simultaneously.

Ingenta

Includes more than 19 million citations for more than 29,000 interdisciplinary journals, including electronic (full-text) delivery. Delivery is sometimes for a fee, or documents may be available for free through your library subscription.

JSTOR

Provides full-text and full-image access to core journals in the humanities, social sciences, and sciences.

Lexis-Nexis Academic

Indexes approximately 5,000 publications, mostly full text, including newspapers, legal news, general interest magazines, medical journals, company financial information, wire service reports, government publications, and more.

ProQuest

Publisher of several databases, including ABI/Inform. Databases can be searched one at a time or simultaneously.

Readers' Guide Abstracts

Indexes popular magazines and periodicals, including abstracts of articles and bibliographical citations.

Research Library (formerly Periodical Abstracts)

Abstracts, indexing, and full-text articles for scholarly journals and general magazines.

SELECTED SPECIALIZED ONLINE DATABASES

Check with your library for a complete list of available databases.

Arts and Humanities

AATA Online (formerly Art and Archaeology Technical Abstracts).
America: History and Life.
Art Index.
GALE Literary Databases.
Grove Art Online.
MLA International Bibliography.
RILM Abstracts of Music Literature.

Biography and General Reference

Academic Search Premier.
African-American Biographical Database.
Book Index with Reviews.
Books in Print.
Biography and Genealogy Master Index.
Dissertation Abstracts at ProQuest.
WorldCat.

Business and Economics

ABI/INFORM Complete.
Business Source Premier.
Ingenta.
LexisNexis Academic.
Mergent Online.

Health and Medicine

AGRICOLA (Agricultural Sciences).
Biological Abstracts.
CINAHL: Nursing and Allied Health.
Health Source: Consumer Edition.

MEDLINE.
NILM (National Library of Medicine).

Science and Technology

Applied Science and Technology Index.
AccessScience@McGraw-Hill.
Biological Abstracts.
Computer and Information Systems Abstracts.
Current Contents.
Ecology Abstracts.
Genetics Abstracts.
GEOBASE.
Mechanical Engineering Abstracts.

Social Sciences

Current Contents.
ERIC.
LexisNexis Academic.
PAIS International.
PsycINFO.
Social Sciences Information Gateway.
Sociological Abstracts.
Westlaw Campus Research.

SEARCH ENGINES AND DIRECTORIES

About.com (http://about.com).
   A network of over 57,000 topics overseen by professional guides.

AltaVista (http://www.altavista.com).
   A whole-Internet search engine that allows for simple keyword
   searches as well as more advanced Boolean search techniques.

Ask Jeeves (http://www.askjeeves.com).

Ask Jeeves, your own "personal butler," your question in plain English and let him do the legwork for you.

CataList (http://www.lsoft.com/lists/listref.html).

The official catalog of listserv lists, including over 74,000 public lists.

Excite (http://www.excite.com).

Excite offers a customizable start page, comprehensive search technology, free email, and more.

Google (http://www.google.com).

In addition to providing easy access to powerful Web page search technology, Google offers specialized engines, such as Google Scholar at http://scholar.google.com and Google Groups at http://groups.google.com, to help you to find exactly what you're looking for.

HotBot (http://www.hotbot.com).

HotBot allows you to build customized filters for your searches using Google or Ask Jeeves engines.

Reference.com (www.reference.com).

Reference.com offers easy access to online reference sources, including dictionaries, almanacs, encyclopedias, literary texts and resources, medical resources, and more.

Social Science Information Gateway (http://sosig.esrc.bris.ac.uk).

Part of the UK's Resource Discovery Network, the SOSIG is a freely available Internet service providing high-quality information in business, law, and the social sciences.

Tile.Net (http://www.tile.net).

Search for email lists, ezines, and newsgroups on a variety of topics.

Webcrawler (http://webcrawler.com).

Webcrawler allows you to choose the parameters for your search, including choosing which search engines and default keywords to use. You can also choose how you want the results sorted by relevance.

Yahoo! (http://www.yahoo.com).
One of the largest search directories on the Web, Yahoo! offers over half a million sites divided into more than 25,000 categories, customizable home pages, and free email.

ONLINE COLLECTIONS

ERIC (http://www.eric.ed.gov).
The Educational Resources Information Center (ERIC), a federally funded national information system that provides—through its subject-specific clearinghouses, associated adjunct clearinghouses, and support components—a variety of services and products on a broad range of education-related issues.

Berkeley Digital Library (http://sunsite.berkeley.edu/Collections).
A digital collection of resources, primarily in literature.

The Electronic Text Center at the University of Virginia (http://etext.lib.virginia.edu).
The Electronic Text Center at the University of Virginia offers an online archive of thousands of electronic texts (most of which are publicly available).

Eserver.org (http://eserver.org).
Eserver has been publishing humanities texts online since 1990. Today it offers almost thirty-five thousand works covering a wide range of interests.

The Labyrinth (http://www.georgetown.edu/labyrinth/labyrinth-home.html).
A World Wide Web server for Medieval Studies sponsored by Georgetown University.

Columbia University's Project Bartleby (http://www.columbia.edu/acis/bartleby).

A searchable site including e-texts, bibliographic records, first-line indexing, and more.

Project Gutenberg (http://www.promo.net/pg).
A collection of electronically available texts, most in the public domain, in a choice of formats.

UMI (http://www.umi.com).
UMI collects and distributes information via microform (both microfilm and microfiche), magnetic tape, paper, CD-ROM, and online, through ProQuest Direct, which enables users with a computer and a **modem**, or an Internet connection, to conveniently access UMI's vast collection of journals, periodicals, magazines, newspapers, and other information sources. The information is available—for a fee—in image, text, and a unique UMI format that combines searchable text with graphs, charts, and photos.

Victorian Women Writers Project (http://www.indiana.edu/~letrs/vwwp).
The goal of the Victorian Women Writers Project is to produce highly accurate transcriptions of literary works by British women writers of the late nineteenth century, encoded using the Standard Generalized Markup Language (SGML). The works, selected with the assistance of an advisory board, include anthologies, novels, political pamphlets, and volumes of poetry and verse drama. Considerable attention is given to accuracy and completeness of texts and to accurate bibliographical descriptions of them.

Voice of the Shuttle (http://vos.ucsb.edu).
A Web site for Humanities research, the Voice of the Shuttle includes highlights and links to a wide variety of sources available online.

Women's Studies Database (http://www.mith2.umd.edu/Womens Studies).

A searchable database of resources in women's studies, maintained by the University of Maryland's Women's Studies Department.

GENERAL REFERENCE SOURCES

Bartlett's Familiar Quotations (http://www.bartleby.com/100).

CIA World Fact Book (http://www.cia.gov/cia/publications/factbook).

Encarta Encyclopedia (http://encarta.msn.com).

Encyclopaedia Britannica (http://www.britannica.com).

Gallup Opinion Polls (http://www.gallup.com).

Roget's Thesaurus II (http://www.bartleby.com/62).

Statistical Abstract of the United States (http://www.census.gov/statab/www).

Thomas Legislative Information (http://thomas.loc.gov).

U.S. Government Printing Office (http://www.access.gpo.gov:80/aboutgpo/index.html).

Merriam-Webster Dictionary (http://www.m-w.com).

Appendix B

FILE EXTENSIONS

File extensions usually consist of three to four letters or numbers after the "dot" in the file name (e.g., cgos.doc). The file extension is created by the "save" feature in most computer applications and tells the computer's operating system which application to use to open the file. There are thousands of file extensions, each associated with a different application or with various properties of an application. Some of the more commonly encountered file extensions are listed below. For a more complete list, visit *Webopedia*'s "Data Formats and Their File Extensions" at http://www.webopedia.com/quick_ref/fileextensions.asp.

File Extension	Application
AI	Adobe *Illustrator* drawing
AIF	Apple/Mac AIFF sound
ANS, ANSI	ANSI Text file
ASP	Active Server Page

AVI	Microsoft Video for Windows movie
BAK, BK	Backup file
BAT	Batch file
BIN	Binary file
BMP	Windows or OS/2 Bitmap file
CDA	CD Audio Track
CDR	Corel *Draw* drawing
CDX	Corel *Draw* compressed drawing
CFG	Configuration file
CGI	Common Gateway Interface script file
CGM	Computer Graphics metafile
CHK	File fragments saved by Windows ScanDisk or Defrag
CLASS	Java file
CLS	Visual Basic class module
CMV	Corel Movie animation
CSS	Cascading Style Sheet datafile/ datasheet
DAT	Data file
DBF	dBase database file
DCR	Shockwave file
DCS	Desktop color separation file
DIB	Device-independent bitmap
DIR	Macromedia *Director* file
DLL	Dynamic-Link library
DOC	Document (Microsoft *Word*, *WordStar*, *FrameMaker* or *FrameBuilder*, *WordPerfect*)
EMF	Enhanced Windows metafile
EPS	Encapsulated PostScript image
EXE	Executable file
FIF	Fractal image file

FLA	Macromedia *Flash* file
FON	System font
FOR	Fortran File
FP	FileMaker Pro file
GIF	CompuServe bitmap file (image)
GRA	Microsoft Graph
GZ	Unix Gzip compressed file
HEX, HQX	Macintosh BinHex file
HGL	HP Graphics language drawing
HLP	Help file
HTM, HTML	Hypertext document file
ICO	Windows icon
INI	Initialization file
JAVA	Java source code
JIF, JFF	JPEG bitmap file
JPG, JPEG	JPEG image file
JS	Javascript source code
LIB	Library
LOG	Log file
MAC	MacPaint image file
MDB	Microsoft *Access* database
MIC	Microsoft *Image Composer* file
MID	MIDI Music file
MMM	Microsoft Multimedia Movie
MOV	*QuickTime for Windows* Movie
MPE, MPG, MPEG	MPEG animation
MP3	MPEG Audio Layer 3 (AC3) file
MSP	Microsoft *Paint* bitmap file
MUS	Music file
OBJ	Object file
ODF	OASIS OpenDocument format for office applications
ODP	OpenDocument Presentation file
ODT	OpenDocument Text file

OLE	OLE Object
PCD	Kodak Photo-CD image
PCL	HP Laserjet bitmap
PCS	PICS animation
PCT	MacIntosh *PICT* drawing
PDF	Adobe Portable Document Format file
PIC	PC *Paint, Lotus,* or MacIntosh *PICT* drawing
PIF	Program information file
PNG	Portable Network Graphics bitmap
PPS	Microsoft *PowerPoint* slide show
PPT	Microsoft *PowerPoint* presentation file
PRE	Lotus *Freelance* presentation file
PRS	*Harvard Graphics for Windows* presentation
PS	PostScript
PUB	Microsoft or Ventura *Publisher* file
QT, QTM	QuickTime movie
QXD	Quark Express file
RA, RAM	*Real Audio* sound file
RAS	Sun Raster Images bitmap
RM	*Real Audio* video file
RMI	MIDI music file
RTF	Rich Text Format file
SHB, SHW	Corel *Show* presentation file
SND	MacIntosh or NeXt sound
SWF	Shockwave Flash object
SYS	System file
TGA	Targa bitmap

TIF, TIFF	Tag Image File Format (TIFF) bitmap image
TMP	Windows temporary file
TTF	TrueType font file
TXT	Text file
URL	Uniform Resource Locator; Internet shortcut file
WAV	Windows Waveform sound
WBK	Microsoft *Word* backup file
WKS	Lotus *1-2-3* spreadsheet file; Microsoft *Works* document file
WP, WPD	*WordPerfect* document
WPG	*WordPerfect* graphic
WPS	Microsoft *Works* document
XLS	Microsoft *Excel* worksheet
Z	Unix Gzip file
ZIP	Zip file

Appendix C

ABBREVIATIONS USED IN WORKS CITED
OR BIBLIOGRAPHIC ENTRIES

Comp., comp.	Compiler, compiled by
Ed., Eds., ed.	Editor, Editors, edited by
Maint., maint.	Maintainer, maintained by
Mod.	Modified
¶	Paragraph (see also para.)
p.	Page
pp.	Pages
para.	Paragraph (see also ¶)
Rev.	Revised
sec.	section
UP	University Press
Vers.	Version

OTHER COMMON ABBREVIATIONS FOR PRESSES, STYLE GUIDES, AND DATABASES

APA	American Psychological Association
CBE	Council of Biology Editors (see also *CSE)*
CGOS	Columbia Guide to Online Style (see also *COS)*
CMS, CMOS	Chicago Manual of Style
COS	Columbia Online Style (see also *CGOS)*
CSE	Council of Science Editors (see also *CBE)*
DAI	*Dissertation Abstracts International*
MLA	Modern Language Association

TWO-LETTER POST OFFICE ABBREVIATIONS: STATES

State/Possession	Abbreviation
Alabama	AL
Alaska	AK
American Samoa	AS
Arizona	AZ
Arkansas	AR
California	CA
Colorado	CO
Connecticut	CT
Delaware	DE
District of Columbia	DC
Federated states of Micronesia	FM
Florida	FL
Georgia	GA
Guam	GU

State/Possession	Abbreviation
Hawaii	HI
Idaho	ID
Illinois	IL
Indiana	IN
Iowa	IA
Kansas	KS
Kentucky	KY
Louisiana	LA
Maine	ME
Marshall Islands	MH
Maryland	MD
Massachusetts	MA
Michigan	MI
Minnesota	MN
Mississippi	MS
Missouri	MO
Montana	MT
Nebraska	NE
Nevada	NV
New Hampshire	NH
New Jersey	NJ
New Mexico	NM
New York	NY
North Carolina	NC
North Dakota	ND
Northern Mariana Islands	MP
Ohio	OH
Oklahoma	OK
Oregon	OR
Palau	PW
Pennsylvania	PA
Puerto Rico	PR

State/Possession	Abbreviation
Rhode Island	RI
South Carolina	SC
South Dakota	SD
Tennessee	TN
Texas	TX
Utah	UT
Vermont	VT
Virgin Islands	VI
Virginia	VA
Washington	WA
West Virginia	WV
Wisconsin	WI
Wyoming	WY

INTERNET COUNTRY CODES

AC	Ascension Island
AD	Andorra
AE	United Arab Emirates
AF	Afghanistan
AG	Antigua and Barbuda
AI	Anguilla
AL	Albania
AM	Armenia
AN	Netherlands Antilles
AO	Angola
AQ	Antarctica
AR	Argentina
AS	American Samoa
AT	Austria
AU	Australia
AW	Aruba
AZ	Azerbaijan

BA	Bosnia and Herzegovina
BB	Barbados
BD	Bangladesh
BE	Belgium
BF	Burkina Faso
BG	Bulgaria
BH	Bahrain
BI	Burundi
BJ	Benin
BM	Bermuda
BN	Brunei Darussalam
BO	Bolivia
BR	Brazil
BS	Bahamas
BT	Bhutan
BV	Bouvet Island
BW	Botswana
BY	Belarus
BZ	Belize
CA	Canada
CC	Cocos (Keeling) Islands
CD	Democratic Republic of Congo (formerly Zaire)
CF	Central African Republic
CG	Congo
CH	Switzerland
CI	Côte D'Ivoire (Ivory Coast)
CK	Cook Islands
CL	Chile
CM	Cameroon
CN	China
CO	Colombia
CR	Costa Rica
CS	Czechoslovakia (former)

CU	Cuba
CV	Cape Verde
CX	Christmas Island
CY	Cyprus
CZ	Czech Republic
DE	Germany
DJ	Djibouti
DK	Denmark
DM	Dominica
DO	Dominican Republic
DZ	Algeria
EC	Ecuador
EE	Estonia
EG	Egypt
EH	Western Sahara
ER	Eritrea
ES	Spain
ET	Ethiopia
FI	Finland
FJ	Fiji
FK	Falkland Islands (Malvinas)
FM	Micronesia
FO	Faroe Islands
FR	France
FX	France, Metropolitan
GA	Gabon
GB	Great Britain (UK)
GD	Grenada
GE	Georgia
GF	French Guiana
GH	Ghana
GI	Gibraltar
GL	Greenland
GM	Gambia

GN	Guinea
GP	Guadeloupe
GQ	Equatorial Guinea
GR	Greece
GS	S. Georgia and S. Sandwich Islands
GT	Guatemala
GU	Guam
GW	Guinea-Bissau
GY	Guyana
HK	Hong Kong
HM	Heard and McDonald Islands
HN	Honduras
HR	Croatia (Hrvatska)
HT	Haiti
HU	Hungary
ID	Indonesia
IE	Ireland
IL	Israel
IN	India
IO	British Indian Ocean Territory
IQ	Iraq
IR	Iran
IS	Iceland
IT	Italy
JM	Jamaica
JO	Jordan
JP	Japan
KE	Kenya
KG	Kyrgyzstan
KH	Cambodia
KI	Kiribati
KM	Comoros
KN	Saint Kitts and Nevis
KP	Korea (North)

KR	Korea (South)
KW	Kuwait
KY	Cayman Islands
KZ	Kazakhstan
LA	Laos
LB	Lebanon
LC	Saint Lucia
LI	Liechtenstein
LK	Sri Lanka
LR	Liberia
LS	Lesotho
LT	Lithuania
LU	Luxembourg
LV	Latvia
LY	Libya
MA	Morocco
MC	Monaco
MD	Moldova
MG	Madagascar
MH	Marshall Islands
MK	Macedonia
ML	Mali
MM	Myanmar
MN	Mongolia
MO	Macau
MP	Northern Mariana Islands
MQ	Martinique
MR	Mauritania
MS	Montserrat
MT	Malta
MU	Mauritius
MV	Maldives
MW	Malawi
MX	Mexico

MY	Malaysia
MZ	Mozambique
NA	Namibia
NC	New Caledonia
NE	Niger
NF	Norfolk Island
NG	Nigeria
NI	Nicaragua
NL	Netherlands
NO	Norway
NP	Nepal
NR	Nauru
NT	Neutral Zone
NU	Niue
NZ	New Zealand (Aotearoa)
OM	Oman
PA	Panama
PE	Peru
PF	French Polynesia
PG	Papua New Guinea
PH	Philippines
PK	Pakistan
PL	Poland
PM	St. Pierre and Miquelon
PN	Pitcairn Island
PR	Puerto Rico
PT	Portugal
PW	Palau
PY	Paraguay
QA	Qatar
RE	Reunion
RO	Romania
RU	Russia
RW	Rwanda

SA	Saudi Arabia
SB	Solomon Islands
SC	Seychelles
SD	Sudan
SE	Sweden
SG	Singapore
SH	St. Helena
SI	Slovenia
SJ	Svalbard and Jan Mayen Islands
SK	Slovak Republic
SL	Sierra Leone
SM	San Marino
SN	Senegal
SO	Somalia
SR	Surinam
ST	Sao Tome and Principe
SV	El Salvador
SY	Syria
SZ	Swaziland
TC	Turks and Caicos Islands
TD	Chad
TF	French Southern Territories
TG	Togo
TH	Thailand
TJ	Tajikistan
TK	Tokelau
TM	Turkmenistan
TN	Tunisia
TO	Tonga
TP	East Timor
TR	Turkey
TT	Trinidad and Tobago
TV	Tuvalu
TW	Taiwan

TZ	Tanzania
UA	Ukraine
UG	Uganda
UK	United Kingdom
UM	U.S. Minor Outlying Islands
US	United States
UY	Uruguay
UZ	Uzbekistan
VA	Vatican City State (Holy See)
VC	Saint Vincent and the Grenadines
VE	Venezuela
VG	Virgin Islands (British)
VI	Virgin Islands (U.S.)
VN	Vietnam
VU	Vanuatu
WF	Wallis and Futuna Islands
WS	Samoa
YE	Yemen
YT	Mayotte
YU	Yugoslavia
ZA	South Africa
ZM	Zambia
ZR	Zaire (now CD, Democratic Republic of Congo)
ZW	Zimbabwe

Appendix D

OTHER DOCUMENTATION STYLES

Columbia Online Style (COS) is designed to work with *any* style simply by translating the elements of a reference to an online or electronically accessed source. First, determine whether the style is a humanities or a scientific style. Next, examine the required elements for the specific style (e.g., Chicago, Turabian, CSE, and so on), and then translate the elements following the examples in chapters 3 and 4. See appendix E for a listing of some of the more commonly used style manuals.

HUMANITIES STYLES

Some styles, such as Chicago (see *The Chicago Manual of Style*, 15th ed.), use footnotes along with an optional bibliography rather than parenthetic notes in the text to document sources. For example, a footnote reference to an article, which has been previously published in print, retrieved from an online database would appear as follows:

1. Author's Name, "Title of Article," *Journal Title* or in *Title of Book*, followed immediately by the original print publication information [if applicable], *Title of Online Database*, publisher information or electronic address including document or file number (if applicable) (date of access, if appropriate).

For example,

1. Ben Corry, "An Energy-Efficient Gating Mechanism in the Acetylcholine Receptor Channel Suggested by Molecular and Brownian Dynamics," *Biophysical Journal* 90 (2006): 799–810, ProQuest, ProQuest Doc. ID #976791001 (22 May 2006).

Bibliographies are optional in Chicago style since the note contains full publication information. However, if you are required to compile a separate bibliography for the previous example, it would appear as follows:

Corry, Ben. "An Energy-Efficient Gating Mechanism in the Acetylcholine Receptor Channel Suggested by Molecular and Brownian Dynamics." *Biophysical Journal* 90 (2006): 799–810. ProQuest. ProQuest Doc. ID #976791001 (22 May 2006).

An item retrieved from the World Wide Web would include the URL, or protocol and Internet address.

2. John G. A. Pocock, "Classical and Civil History: The Transformation of Humanism," *Cromohs* 1 (1996): 1–34, http://www.unifi.it/riviste/cromohs/1_96/pocock.html (1 May 2006).

The bibliographic entry would follow the same logic:

Pocock, John G. A. "Classical and Civil History: The Transformation of Humanism." *Cromohs* 1 (1996): 1–34. http://www.unifi.it/riviste/cromohs/1_96/pocock.html (1 May 2006).

SCIENTIFIC STYLES

Scientific styles, such as the Council of Science Editors (CSE) style (formerly known as the Council of Biology Editors [CBE] style), also use superscripted numbers in the text, in this case keyed to a list of sources (usually titled "References"), similar to APA style. Note that Columbia Online Style omits the "Available from:" statement from the entry.

A typical CSE entry for an electronic source, following Columbia Online Style, might appear as follows:

1. Roccheri MC, Onorato K, Tipa C, Casano C. EGTA treatment causes the synthesis of heat shock proteins in sea urchin embryos. Mol Cell Biol Res Comm [Internet]. 2000; 3(5):306–311. *Science Direct.com.* Elsevier. http://www.sciencedirect.com/science/journal/15224724 (23 Dec. 2005).

Appendix E

SELECTED BIBLIOGRAPHY

The ACS Style Guide: A Manual for Authors and Editors. 2nd ed. Ed. Janet S. Dodd. Washington, D.C.: American Chemical Society, 1997.

AIP Style Manual. 4th ed. New York: American Institute of Physics, 1990–1997. http://www.aip.org/pubservs/style/4thed/toc.html.

ALWD Citation Manual: A Professional System of Citation. 2nd ed. Ed. Association of Legal Writing Directors and Darby Dickerson. Gaithersburg, Md.: Aspen Law and Business, 2004.

American Medical Association Manual of Style. 9th ed. Ed. Cheryl Iverson. Baltimore, Md.: Williams and Wilkins, 1998.

ASM Style Manual for Journals and Books. Washington, D.C.: American Society for Microbiology, 1992.

The Associated Press Stylebook and Briefing on Media Law. Rev. ed. Ed. Norm Goldstein. Reading, Mass.: Perseus Books, 2002.

The Bluebook: A Uniform System of Citation. 18th ed. Cambridge, Mass.: Harvard Law Review Association, 2001.

Canadian Guide to Uniform Legal Citation. 5th ed. Scarborough, Ont.: McGill Law Journal, 2002.

The Chicago Manual of Style. 15th ed. Chicago: University of Chicago Press, 2003.

CNS Stylebook on Religion: A Reference Guide and Usage Manual 3rd ed. Washington, D.C.: Catholic News Service, 2006.

The Complete Guide to Citing Government Information Resources: A Manual for Writers and Librarians. Rev. ed. Ed. Diane L. Garner and Diane H. Smith. Bethesda, Md.: American Library Association Government Documents Round Table, 1993.

The Elements of Legal Style. 2nd ed. By Bryan A. Garner. New York: Oxford University Press, 2002.

Information and Documentation—Bibliographic References, Part 2, Electronic Documents or Parts Thereof. International Standards Organization (ISO). ISO #690–2. New York: American National Standards Institute (ANSI), 2002. http://www.nlc-bnc. ca/iso/tc46sc9/standard/690-2e.htm.

The Elements of Style. 4th ed. By William Strunk Jr., and E. B. White. Boston: Allyn and Bacon, 2000.

Franklin Covey Style Guide for Business and Technical Communication. By Franklin Covey. Salt Lake City, Utah: Ingram-LaVergne, 2000.

Gregg Reference Manual. 10th ed. By William A. Sabin. New York: McGraw-Hill/Irwin, 2005.

A Manual for Authors of Mathematical Papers. Rev. ed. Providence, R.I.: American Mathematical Society, 1990.

A Manual for Writers of Term Papers, Theses, and Dissertation. 6th ed. By Kate L. Turabian. Chicago: University of Chicago Press, 1996.

MLA Style Manual and Guide to Scholarly Publishing. 2nd ed. Ed. Joseph Gibaldi. New York: Modern Language Association, 1998.

The New York Public Library Writer's Guide to Style and Usage. By Andrea Sutcliffe. New York: HarperResource, 1994.

The New York Times Manual of Style and Usage. Rev. ed. Ed. Allan M. Siegal and William G. Connolly. New York: Times Books, 2002.

The Oxford Guide to Style. 2nd ed. Ed. Robert Ritter. New York: Oxford University Press, 2002.

Publication Manual of the American Psychological Association. 5th ed. Washington, D.C.: American Psychological Association, 2001.

SBL Handbook of Style: For Ancient Near Eastern, Biblical, and Early Christian Studies. Ed. Patrick H. Alexander et al. Peabody, Mass.: Hendrickson, 1999.

Scientific Style and Format: The CSE Manual for Authors, Editors, and Publishers. 7th ed. Style Manual Committee of the Council of Science Editors. Cambridge: Cambridge University Press, 2006.

Style Manual for Political Science. Rev. ed. Washington, D.C.: American Political Science Association Committee on Publications, 2001.

Suggestions to Authors of the Reports of the United States Geological Survey. 7th ed. Ed. Wallace R. Hansen. Washington, D.C.: U.S. Government Printing Office, 1991.

"The Times" Guide to English Style and Usage. Rev. ed. Ed. Tim Austin. New York: HarperCollins, 1999.

United States Government Printing Office Style Manual 2000. Washington, D.C.: U.S. Government Printing Office, 2000.

The Wall Street Journal Essential Guide to Business Style and Usage. Ed. Paul R. Martin. New York: Free Press, 2003.

Wikipedia: Manual of Style. http://en.wikipedia.org/wiki/Wikipedia:Manual_of_Style

Writing About Music: A Style Sheet from the Editors of "Nineteenth-Century Music." By D. Kern Holoman. Berkeley: University of California Press, 1988.

Appendix F

Character	Decimal	Entity Reference	Character	Decimal	Entity Reference
NUL	0		SOH	1	
STX	2		ETX	3	
EOT	4		ENQ	5	
ACK	6		BEL	7	
BS	8		HT	9	
LF	10		VT	11	
NP	12		CR	13	
SO	14		SI	15	
DLE	16		DC1	17	
DC2	18		DC3	19	
DC4	20		NAK	21	
SYN	22		ETB	23	
CAN	24		EM	25	
SUB	26		ESC	27	
FS	28		GS	29	
RS	30		US	31	
SP	32		!	33	
"	34	"	#	35	
$	36		%	37	
&	38	&	'	39	
(	40		)	41	

Character	Decimal	Entity Reference	Character	Decimal	Entity Reference
*	42		+	43	
,	44		-	45	
.	46		/	47	
0	48		1	49	
2	50		3	51	
4	52		5	53	
6	54		7	55	
8	56		9	57	
:	58		;	59	
<	60	&lt;	=	61	
>	62	&gt;	?	63	
@	64		A	65	
B	66		C	67	
D	68		E	69	
F	70		G	71	
H	72		I	73	
J	74		K	75	
L	76		M	77	
N	78		O	79	
P	80		Q	81	
R	82		S	83	
T	84		U	85	
V	86		W	87	
X	88		Y	89	
Z	90		[	91	
\	92		]	93	
^	94		_	95	
`	96		a	97	
b	98		c	99	
d	100		e	101	
f	102		g	103	

Character	Decimal	Entity Reference	Character	Decimal	Entity Reference
h	104		i	105	
j	106		k	107	
l	108		m	109	
n	110		o	111	
p	112		q	113	
r	114		s	115	
t	116		u	117	
v	118		w	119	
x	120		y	121	
z	122		{	123	
|	124		}	125	
~	126		DEL	127	
	160		¡	161	&iexcl;
¢	162	&cent;	£	163	&pound;
¤	164	&curren;	¥	165	&yen;
|	166	&brvbar;	§	167	&sect;
¨	168	&uml;	©	169	&copy;
ª	170	&ordf;	«	171	&laquo;
¬	172	&not;		173	&shy;
®	174	&reg;	–	175	&hibar;
°	176	&deg;	±	177	&plusmn;
²	178	&sup2;	³	179	&sup3;
´	180	&acute;	:	181	&micro;
¶	182	&para;	·	183	&middot;
¸	184	&cedil;	¹	185	&sup1;
º	186	&ordm;	»	187	&raquo;
¼	188	&frac14;	½	189	&frac12;
¾	190	&frac34;	¿	191	&iquest;
À	192	&Agrave;	Á	193	&Aacute;
Â	194	&Acirc;	Ã	195	&Atilde;
Ä	196	&Auml;	Å	197	&Aring;

Character	Decimal	Entity Reference	Character	Decimal	Entity Reference
Æ	198	Æ	Ç	199	Ç
È	200	È	É	201	É
Ê	202	Ê	Ë	203	Ë
Ì	204	Ì	Í	205	Í
Î	206	Î	Ï	207	Ï
Ð	208	ð	Ñ	209	&Ntidle;
Ò	210	Ò	Ó	211	Ó
Ô	212	Ô	Õ	213	Õ
Ö	214	Ö	×	215	×
Ø	216	Ø	Ù	217	Ù
Ú	218	Ú	Û	219	Û
Ü	220	Ü	Ý	221	Ý
Þ	222	þ	ß	223	ß
à	224	à	á	225	á
â	226	â	ã	227	ã
ä	228	ä	å	229	å
æ	230	æ	ç	231	ç
è	232	è	é	233	é
ê	234	ê	ë	235	ë
ì	236	ì	í	237	í
î	238	î	ï	239	ï
ð	240	ð	ñ	241	ñ
ò	242	ò	ó	243	ó
ô	244	ô	õ	245	õ
ö	246	ö	÷	247	÷
ø	248	ø	ù	249	ù
ú	250	ú	û	251	û
ü	252	ü	ý	253	ý
þ	254	þ	ÿ	255	ÿ

Address. The location of a specific site or document, usually including the domain name and the path to access a particular file.

Alias. Many Internet sites and electronic mail configurations allow the user to designate an alias or fictitious name. Many electronic mail programs also use a login name rather than the user's actual name in mail headers. Programs such as MOOs and MUDs and chat rooms (*which see*) usually allow the user to select a character name to use. When an author's name is not available, the alias may be used instead.

American Standard Code for Information Interchange (ASCII). A sevenbit code representing 128 characters that is capable of translating letters, numbers, and special characters across a wide variety of platforms. *See also* **ISO Latin-1**.

Anchors. Hypertext tags used to create links. In addition to linking to external documents or files, anchors can link to specific actions within the same document or file by specifying anchor names within a document.

Applet. A program written in Java scripting language that can be included in an HTML file by using the <APPLET CODE = > . . . </APPLET> tags to call up the program from a discret location. *See also* Java, Javascript.

Angle brackets. Symbols (< >) used in Hypertext Markup Language to designate hypertext commands. They should not be used around URLs or email addresses as they may cause confusion with software applications and add unnecessary complexity.

Archive. A location where files or collections of files are stored for later access. Many WWW archives are searchable and use various download and compression protocols, depending on the site and the types of files stored.

ASCII (*see* **American Standard Code for Information Interchange**).

BBS (*see* **Bulletin Board Service**).

Binary code. A system of numbers with only two digits (1s and 0s) used by digital computers to represent information.

Blog. Short for Web log, a blog is the name given to an automatically generated Web page consisting of, usually, brief messages or entries. Many blogs are similar to personal journals or diaries but may include links or graphics.

Bookmarks. A way of marking specific files, Web page addresses, or locations in a file for later retrieval. *See also* **Favorites**.

Boolean operators. Used by many Internet and library search engines and databases, these are operators such as "AND," "OR," "NOT," or "NEAR" that limit or define search terms in a query. For example, "movies OR films" returns a list of all documents or Web pages found that contain either term; "films NOT movies" returns a list of only those sites that do not include the word "movies."

Boolean searches. A library, database, or Web search that uses Boolean operators (*which see*).

Broadband. A type of data transmission using a single wire to transmit several channels at the same time. Broadband connections allow for the transfer of data between computers at a much faster rate than traditional dial-in services.

Browser. A software program that allows users to access the World Wide Web and move through hypertextual links. Some browsers, such as *Lynx*, offer text-only versions, while browsers such as Netscape *Communicator* or Microsoft's *Internet Explorer* offer graphical interfaces and use point-and-click technology.

Bulletin Board Service (BBS). A service that provides access (usually dial-in) to remote users, enabling them to access files and information and to communicate with other users. Files reside on the host computer and can be shared and downloaded by authorized users. Most BBSs require the user to obtain an account on the service, either for free or for a fee. BBSs may be small, consisting of only a dozen or so users, or extremely large, with millions of subscribers. Many BBSs offer subscribers varying levels of Internet access as well.

CD-ROM. Compact Disc, Read-Only Memory. An electronic storage medium designed to hold large amounts of information.

CGI. Common Gateway Interface. A scripting language that allows hypertext documents to be customized and documents produced, usually in real time, in response to user input.

Chat room. Any of several synchronous, real-time communication sites that allow users to connect and communicate with one another, usually by inputting text or commands on a keyboard. Some chat rooms also allow for the use of real-time audio and video conferencing, file exchanges, and other features.

Client. A client is a software program installed on the host computer or on the user's personal computer that facilitates certain protocols. Client programs are available for various platforms for FTP, gopher, telnet, email, synchronous communications, and a wide array of other common online uses.

Common Gateway Interface (*see* **CGI**).

Compact Disc, Read-only Memory (*see* **CD-ROM**).

Courseware. A term often used to designate software designed specifically for educational purposes, such as WebCT or Blackboard. Often, courseware includes presentation space for documents and files, quizzes, grade reporting, and messaging in the form of asynchronous discussion forums (similar to email) or real-time chat spaces.

Cyberspace. A term coined by William Gibson in his cyberpunk novel *Neuromancer* to refer to the entire online world, the computerized space in which programs and files reside and communication takes place.

Database. A collection of files, usually containing common fields or data records, that allows data to be organized, searched, and manipulated for use in various ways.

Digital. Generally used to designate information, files, and other media stored or accessed in binary code (*which see*).

Digital Subscriber Lines (DSL). A type of digital network connection that uses traditional telephone lines but allows for high-speed data transmission.

Directory. A structure for organizing files on a computer or host, similar to a file folder or drawer containing individual documents.

Disc (*see* **CD-ROM**).

Disk (*see* **diskette**).

Diskette. A computer storage medium, nowadays usually 3.5-inch, high-density, and capable of storing 1.44 MB of data. Also sometimes called disks, floppy disks, or just plain "floppies."

DNS (*see* **Domain Name Server**).

Document-type definitions (DTDs). A system of tags used to mark up a document or file used to describe the content rather than the appearance of elements in the document or file. *See also* **markup languages**.

Domain, domain name. The unique alias for a specific IP (*which see*) address that is used to connect to an individual site or page on the Internet.

Domain Name Server (DNS). This refers to the host machine or computer that provides storage and access to files for a particular domain name.

DOS. Disk Operating System. Software that controls the computer's operation. Other operating systems include Windows, MacIntosh, Linux, and UNIX.

Download. Transfer of information or files from a server to a local host or personal computer.

DSL (*see* **Digital Subscriber Lines**).

DTDs (*see* **Document-type definitions**).

E-books. An electronic or digital version of a book, often using a specific proprietary format that may require certain hardware or software.

Electronic mail (see email).

Email. Electronic mail. A system that allows users to send messages on the Internet or through other electronic systems using modems and telephone lines or cables or some other kind of connection to a server. On most systems, messages are received almost instantaneously and can be read and replied to entirely online.

Ethernet. A means of connecting computers in a network that uses cables for communication. Because they provide direct access, Ethernet connections to an ISP (*which see*) are much faster than dial-in services.

Extensible Markup Language (XML). A version of SGML (*which see*) that allows Web page designers to create customized tags to define functionality. *See also* **Document-type definitions**.

Favorites. In Microsoft *Internet Explorer*, a collection of Web page addresses marked for later retrieval. *See also* **Bookmarks**. Bookmarks and Favorites files can often be organized into folders and may include customizable descriptions as well.

File. A single electronic program, document, image, or element with a discrete name.

File compression. A method of reducing file sizes by encoding their contents. Compressing files allows for faster transmission times.

File extension. Usually, three or four letters (more or less) following the file name and a "dot" (".") that designate the type of file, allowing most operating systems to automatically recognize the file type so that the file can be opened used the appropriate software application.

File Transfer Protocol (FTP). A means of moving files between remote machines.

Flash. A type of vector-graphic animation technology.

Frames. On Web sites, frames are designated HTML elements that permit certain information to be retained onscreen in the browser window while other Web pages are accessed within the frame's borders.

FTP (*see* **File Transfer Protocol**).

GIF. Graphics Interchange Format. A commercial graphics format widely used for images on the Web. *See also* **JPEG, MPEG.**

Google. One of many Internet search engines, Google is such a popular choice that it has become a verb (to "google" something is to search for it using the Google search engine).

Gopher. A menu-driven system for organizing and accessing files and programs on the Internet.

Graphics Interchange Format (*see* **GIF**).

Hanging indent. Used in word processing to designate paragraphs or other text in which the second or subsequent lines are indented while the first line is flush with the left-hand margin. Bibliographic entries are usually formatted using the automatic hanging-indent feature of the word processing application.

Haptic. A term used to refer to the emerging technology that allows for the encoding and transmission of touch.

Hard copy. A paper printout of a file or document stored electronically.

Hard page break. A word-processing command that forces a page break. Pressing the *CTRL* and *ENTER* keys simultaneously creates a hard page break in most word-processing programs.

Hard return. A command that ends one line of text and begins a new one, typically used to end one paragraph and begin a new one in word processors and HTML files. A single hard return is created by pressing the ENTER key once in most word-processing programs. *See also* **soft return.**

Hardware. Physical computer equipment and peripherals, as opposed to the programs or instructions that run on the computer. *See also* **software.**

Headers (*see* **Title bar**).

Home page. The main page for a Web site, usually the default file, or index page, in a particular domain and/or directory.

Host. A computer that allows one or more users on a network to share resources and files.

HTML (*see* **Hypertext Markup Language**).

HTTP (*see* **Hypertext Transfer Protocol**).

Hypermedia. Hypertext documents or files that contain multimedia elements, such as graphics, audio, or video files, as well as texts.

Hypertext. A term used to designate text in electronic files formatted as a link to other information. Also used to refer to documents published electronically that are formatted using Hypertext Markup Language, or HTML.

Hypertext Markup Language (HTML). A language used to create World Wide Web documents that allows the author to include links and other features such as graphics that may be read using Hypertext Transfer Protocol (*which see*).

Hypertext Transfer Protocol (HTTP). The process by which hypertext files, such as pages on the World Wide Web, are transferred between computers on the Internet.

Internet. An international network of computers originally designed by the U.S. Department of Defense to ensure communication abilities in the event of a catastrophe. The Internet today connects millions of individual users, universities, governments, businesses, and organizations, using telephone lines, fiber-optic cabling, Ethernet connections, and other means. The Internet is different from an internet (small *i*), which is any interconnected network of computers.

Internet protocol (IP). The method used to route packets of information using the best available route. The Internet was designed as a means of ensuring communication in the event of a catastrophe. Thus should one route become unavailable or disabled, IP addressing will immediately reroute the information.

Internet service provider (ISP). A service that allows users to connect to the Internet, usually through dial-up or broadband connections.

Intranet. An interconnected network of computers, usually within a single organization, similar to a LAN or WAN. Intranets allow users to share files and communicate with one another using browsers, email, and other applications designed for Internet communication. Intranets may allow access to the Internet; however, they cannot be accessed from outside without a password or account of some kind and thus provide a measure of security for their users.

IP (*see* **Internet protocol**).

ISP (*see* **Internet service provider**).

ISO. International Standards Organization. An international organization in Geneva, Switzerland, dedicated to developing standards for the open exchange of information across different terminals, computers, networks, and applications.

ISO Latin-1. An eight-bit character set, similar to ASCII, that allows 256 characters instead of the 128 characters allowed by he seven-bit code. *See also* **ASCII**.

Java. An object-oriented programming language, similar to C++, that allows users to include programs, called "applets" (*which see*), that can be transferred along with other elements in a hypertextual file to Java-enabled browsers.

Javascript. An object-oriented scripting language used by some Web pages that allows for features other than static text and graphics to be included in a file and interpreted by a browser or other software application.

Joint Photographic Experts Group (see JPEG).

JPEG. Joint Photographic Experts Group. A standard for photographic-quality image compression on the Web. *See also* GIF, MPEG.

Keywords. Designated terms in a document or file that can be searched for using Internet search engines, database search engines, or computerized library catalogs. Usually, keywords represent terms or phrases that are key, or main ideas in the article or file.

LAN (*see* **Local Area Network**).

Library catalog. Nowadays, usually a searchable online database that lists a specific library or consortium of participating libraries' holdings—books, periodicals, media, and other material—that can be searched by keyword, subject, author, or title searches, or by other terms.

Link. A "hot spot" in a hypertext document or file that has been coded to connect the reader to another location within the document or file or to another document or file.

Listproc. A program that allows electronic mail messages directed to a designated address to be sent automatically to all subscribers. *See also* **Listserv, MajorDomo**.

Listserv. Similar to Listproc, this is a type of software that allows electronic mail messages directed to a designated address to be sent automatically to all subscribers to the list. While not entirely accurate, many users use the term "listserv" generically to refer to all types of Internet mailing lists. *See also* **Listproc, MajorDomo.**

Local Area Network (LAN). Two or more computers linked together, usually in close physical proximity, and sharing resources, such as printers or directory space, allocated by a host computer.

Location bar. The text-input area usually located near the top of Internet-browser software's display, where the location, or Internet address, of a particular Web site or file is typed and displayed.

Login name. The name or combination of characters used to designate the person or entity entitled to access a particular site or file. Also called the "user name" or "ID."

Lynx. A text-only browser that allows users to view files on the Web using standard text features. Typographical elements such as fonts, emphasis, and colors and features such as tables and graphics are stripped from the files; however, users may download graphics and other multimedia elements for viewing in other applications.

MajorDomo. One of several types of programs that allow mailing lists to be set up and maintained to support the dissemination of electronic mail messages to subscribers. *See also* **Listproc, Listserv.**

Markup languages. Usually, any of a variety of systems of tags, including HTML, XML, DTD, et al., used to designate specific attributes of a document or file, such as the appearance of elements (e.g., bold, underlined, etc.) or the function of elements (e.g., title, author, etc.).

Medium (plural, media). The means of storing, representing, or communicating information, for instance, digital media, mass media (newspapers, television, etc.), visual media (works of art, photographs, etc.).

Metatags. Special tags, usually in the "head" of a document or file, that provide information about the contents of the file. In HTML documents, metatags may include information about the author, the date of creation, keywords, or other information designated by the author of the page or, sometimes, automatically generated by the software used to author the file, which may be viewed by using the "View Page Source" or "View Source" command in the Web browser.

Mirrors. Sites that copy (or "mirror") information originally posted or published on another site. Mirrors are usually created in order to limit traffic on the original site or to foster quicker access to information from a remote site.

Modem. Modulate/Demodulate. A hardware device that converts data from analog to digital or from digital to analog, thus allowing communication of electronic files between computers using standard telephone lines designed for voice communication.

MOO. MUD, Object Oriented. A form of MUD (*which see*), used for role-playing games, synchronous conferencing, and distance education applications.

Motion Picture Experts Group (*see* **MPEG**).

Mouseover. An effect created using javascript (*which see*) that changes the appearance or action of parts of a Web page simply by moving the mouse over the designated portion of the page. Mouseovers (also called rollovers) are often used effectively for menu items, with the portion of the image changing color, for instance, when the mouse is moved over it.

MPEG. Motion Picture Experts Group. A standard for the compression of video files. *See also* **GIF, JPEG.**

MUD. Multi-User Dungeon, Domain, or Dimension. A game form similar to the *Dungeons and Dragons* role-playing game but originally developed for multiple users on the Internet. Forms of MUDs include MOOs (*which see*), MUSEs, MUCKs, etc.

MUD, Object Oriented (*see* **MOO**).

Multimedia. A mixture of various types of media, including audio, video, graphics, and text.

Multi-User Dungeon, Domain, or Dimension (*see* **MUD**).

Name anchor. In HTML, a reference to a specific location within a document or Web page, usually referred to in the address by a pound sign (#) and reference name or keyword directly following the address of the document, designated in HTML by the tags <A Name = " ">... </A>.

Net (*see* **Internet**). Short for the Internet, hence the initial capital letter.

Newsgroups. Usenet newsgroups allows for messages from many senders to be stored on a specific site for search and retrieval by any interested readers. Unlike listservs and mailing lists, newsgroup messages are not usually delivered to reader's mailboxes and do not usually require subscription.

Offline. Generally, used to refer to the state during which a computer is not connected to or sharing information on a network. Also used to refer to information not available over a network, such as files residing on a local hard drive or disk.

Online. The state during which a computer is connected to or sharing information or programs with another computer or a server. Also sometimes used to designate any work or information on a computer. Online should not be hyphenated.

Page (*see* **Web page**).

PDF (*see* **Portable Document Format**).

Podcast. A multimedia file distributed over the Internet for playback on computers or mobile devices such as iPODs or various mp3 players.

Portable Document Format (PDF). A file format, created by Adobe, that allows for the sharing of documents across platforms, by using a system to describe the format and contents, including text, graphics, and other features.

Port. A number that identifies a specific channel or access location at a given IP address.

Portal. Generally used to refer to a starting point, or gateway, to other resources, such as the Web portal or Web page a library may offer to allow users to access subscriber databases online.

Protocol. A set of rules agreed upon for performing various tasks on the Internet. Common protocols include File Transfer Protocol (FTP), HyperText Transfer Protocol (HTTP), gopher protocols, and telnet protocols.

Search engine. A program that allows users to search for information or files at various locations using keyword searches and, often, Boolean operators. Some search engines search specific sites or types of files; other search engines will search all information on the Internet

Search terms. Often used synonymously with "keywords," search terms are the combination of words or phrases, usually joined with Boolean operators (*which see*) used to locate information in databases or search engines.

Serials. Publications that are issued on a regular basis. Most periodical publications (e.g., newspapers, magazines, journals, etc.) may be collectively referred to as serials.

Server. A computer, or host, that allocates resources and supports the sharing of information or peripherals (such as printers) among various computers on a network.

Service provider (*see* **Internet service provider**).

SGML. Standard Generalized Markup Language. An international standard for formatting a text. SGML is particularly useful for the electronic storage and transmission of files across platforms because it is system- and device-independent.

Signature file. Used to designate name, address, or other contact information that can be created, stored, and automatically appended to the end of email messages.

Sites (*see* **Web site**).

Soft return. A return that a word processor inserts automatically at the end of the line when the text on that line reaches the right-hand margin. Users should not rely on soft returns to end paragraphs and begin new ones. *See also* **hard return**.

Software. Usually, a computer program that instructs the system to perform certain actions to input, retrieve, manipulate, process, output, or store data items. Software controls the operating environment and provides an interface for the user to communicate with the computer in various ways.

Source code. The underlying programming code, usually in human-readable language, used to communicate between software and hardware devices, for example, the system of HTML tags that instruct a Web browser in how to display the text and other features of a Web page.

Standard Generalized Markup Language (*see* **SGML**).

Subdirectory. A directory or folder contained within another directory or folder. Internet addresses often begin with a domain name (the top level), often followed by a directory and one or more subdirectories, usually separated by the forward-slash mark ("/"), and, usually, ending with the name of a specific file within the domain, directory, or subdirectory.

Telnet. An Internet protocol that permits remote access to programs that reside on another computer. Telnet sites may require the user to have an account on the host machine; many telnet sites also allow for guest accounts.

Title bar. In many Windows applications, including popular Internet browsers such as Netscape, Mozilla, and *Internet Explorer*, the title bar refers to the bar (usually blue) at the top of the application window where information about the file or page being viewed is displayed.

Uniform Resource Locator (URL). The Internet address used by browser software to connect to sites on the World Wide Web. A URL usually includes a designation of the protocol, a domain name, directories and subdirectories, and a file name, including a file extension which tells the software how to read and display the information.

UNIX. An operating system used by many Internet host machines that accommodates multiple users and multitasking.

Upload. The process of transferring or moving a file or document from a local host (e.g., a personal computer's hard drive or disk) to a remote server.

URL (*see* **Uniform Resource Locator**).

Virtual Reality Modeling Language (see VRML).

VRML. Virtual Reality Modeling Language. A language used to encode and communicate three-dimensional graphics files among various platforms. It requires a VRML-enabled browser, that is, a browser capable of recognizing and responding to VRML commands.

WAN (*see* **Wide Area Network**).

Web (*see* **World Wide Web**). Short for the World Wide Web, hence the capital "W."

Web browser (*see* **Browser**).

Web page. A document or file on the World Wide Web with a single URL, regardless of its length.

Web server (*see* **server**).

Web site. A specific location or a specific group of related files, usually within a single directory or subdirectory, on the World Wide Web.

Wide Area Network (WAN). Similar to a LAN, a network of computers linked together to share information, files, programs, or hardware and served by a host machine, usually a minicomputer or mainframe, that allocates resources. Unlike LANs, however, WANs often link computers over a large geographic area, including worldwide links. Unlike the Internet, however, WANs are limited to use only by employees or other persons authorized to access the server. *See also* **intranet**.

Wiki. A specific type of collaboratively authored Web document, from the Hawaiian term, "wiki wiki" meaning "super fast."

Word processor. Usually, a specific software application that allows for input, editing, and display of textual and other elements used to produce documents and files for print.

World Wide Web (WWW). Also known simply as the Web, the various forms of documents and files transmitted on the Internet and capable of being accessed by a browser. The World Wide Web is not the same thing as the Internet but rather a user-friendly system of organizing information on the Internet for remote access.

WWW (*see* **World Wide Web**).

WYSIWYG. Pronounced "wizzy-wig"; stands for "What You See Is What You Get." Used to describe applications, such as most current word processors and many Web-authoring programs, that allow users to see the document as it will appear on the final page or screen.

XHTML. Extensible HTML, a more structured standard markup language than regular HTML, which facilitates delivery of content to multiple devices, such as PDAs, mobile phones, and Web-based systems.

XML (*see* **Extensible Markup Language**).

Index